# Wine Roads of France

Frederick Tingey

**Charles Letts & Co Ltd**
**London, Edinburgh & New York**

# Contents

First published 1977
by Charles Letts & Company Limited
Diary House, Borough Road, London SE1 1DW

Designer: Richard Brown Associates
Cover: Richard Brown Associates
Photographs:
French Government Tourist Office, pp 8, 25, 26, 64, 72
Food from France, London, pp 17, 18, 46
Ronald Sheridan, London, p 52
Maps: Anita Tingey

© Text: Frederick Tingey
ISBN 0 85097 176 4

Printed in Great Britain by
Letts Erskine Limited, Dalkeith

# Champagne

Nearly a million visitors tour the cellars of the great champagne houses in Reims and Epernay each year, yet relatively few of them go on to explore the delicate countryside from which this most famous of all sparkling wine comes – even though it is only a stone's throw from the *route nationale* down which many tourists drive on their way south.

Derived from the medieval-French *champaine* (open plain) and *champaign* (battlefield), the modern word Champagne combines both meanings, since the flatlands stretching north, east, and west of Reims have for centuries been a thoroughfare for invading armies – the first led by Attila the Hun, the last by Rommel. In contrast to the plain adjoining them, the vine-clad slopes contribute some of the most inviting autumn scenery in the north of France.

Of the 44,000 acres planted with vines in Champagne the most important parts are the horseshoe-shaped Montagne south of Reims, the Côte des Blancs below Epernay, and the Rivière or valley of the Marne which runs east-west to separate the two. This higher ground, the ancient cliffs of the Ile de France, covers vast deposits of chalk, the fossilized residue of a primeval sea. The vines push their roots several yards deep into the chalk which is burrowed into lower down by over 120 miles of cellars. This is where the champagne is matured and stored.

Covering much the same amount of ground as Paris, this is one of the most concentrated wine districts in the world, where land producing a *premier grand cru* or top quality vintage will fetch £12,000 or more an acre. The only species of vine authorised in Champagne are the *cépages nobles* of Meunier Noir, Pinot Noir, and Chardonnay; the last two – the classic grapes of Burgundy – have been in use since medieval times. But while there have been vineyards in the region since the Gauls planted them on the Montagne in pre-Roman days, champagne as we know it did not exist until the 17th century.

There is a mistaken belief that Dom Perignon, the monk appointed cellar master of the Abbey of Hautvillers near Epernay in 1668, was the inventor of champagne. It is true that he was the first to mix the wines of different vineyards – using a coarse vintage, for example, to give body to a more delicate one – and the first to add a syrup to the blend to make sure it would ferment again in the bottle, but it was the English who were the innovators of the sparkle. In the early-17th century the still white wine of the region frequently underwent a secondary fermentation in the spring, a phenomenon the Champenois did nothing to encourage or prevent. But once the English shippers discovered that their customers liked their wine sparkling they demanded bubbles in all the champagne they imported.

Each of the three great vineyard areas produces a recognisably individual wine: robust and full bodied from the Montagne, fruity and with a powerful bouquet from the Marne valley, and delicate and fresh from the Côte des Blancs. How the champagne houses blend these together determines the taste of their champagne. When the Romans conquered Gaul they extended the vineyards already planted in Champagne, so much so that in AD92 the Emperor Diocletian ordered them to be uprooted, a decision only reversed two centuries later by Probus. Over the years, the monks of the monasteries improved the quality of the wine – then red and still. In the 11th century the wine grew in popularity; even the kings of France and England owned vineyards in the region. By about 1650 the Champenois, taking note of changing tastes, had learned how to make the wine pale and tawny rather than red.

The *vin nature* or still wine of Champagne, only recently allowed to be exported again, now comes in red, rosé, and white; but it is not made every year. One reason why champagne is expensive is that every fourth winter the thin topsoil in the vineyards, washed away by the autumn rains, has to be replaced, usually by hand. Another is the time lost in replanting the vines every 25 to 30 years compared with 80 farther south in the Rhône valley at Châteauneuf du Pape. The old vines are uprooted and the land left fallow for a couple of years. Then there is a wait of four years before the new vines bear fruit. Since the wine from the grapes takes at least three years to mature, it is nine years before they provide any income. Although there may be 16,500 vineyard owners in Champagne, tending their vines is a secondary occupation for many.

Champagne is even more of a wine democracy than Burgundy. There are over 140 *négociants* or champagne houses, though the 13 *grandes marques* own about 15 per cent of the vineyards and produce two-thirds of all the champagne sold. Most growers sell their crop to the *négociants,* getting an average of 50p for every 2 lb of grapes. There are about 125 *co-operatives,* but some 3,000 growers market their wine themselves. They are called *révoltants manipulants,* denoted by the letters RM on the label. Compared with one of the big champagne houses selling five million bottles a year their production may be modest, yet one bottle in four comes from these *petits propriétaires.* Unlike the blends of the champagne houses, these are single-vineyard wines, ie. if the grower names the commune on the bottle label, then that must be the sole place-of-origin of the wine. This *champagne de cru* is in the tradition of a hundred or more years ago, when the wine was sold with the name of a particular growth – as some wines still are. The need for the champagne houses to produce consistent blends gradually led them away from the specific wines of Sillery, Ay, and Mailly. Since 1919, vineyards in Champagne have been officially classified for quality. At the top are the 12 *premiers grands crus,* rated 100 per cent since they are used each year as the yardstick for fixing the maximum price the *négociants* pay for grapes. Next best are the 30 *grands crus,* with ratings of between 90 and 99 per cent. A grower in one of these districts making his own wine has the right to put *premier grand cru* or *grand cru* on the label.

Harvesting begins at the end of September, a hundred days after the flowering. Each bunch of grapes is examined and any imperfect ones rejected. A maximum yield per acre is fixed by law each year and any grapes in excess of this must be set aside. Dotted about the vineyards are *vendangeoirs* where the grape pickers live at harvest time and where the grapes are pressed as soon as they arrive. The grapes are put into wide shallow presses designed to ensure that the juice will not become coloured by the skins. Each press takes 8,800 lb of grapes and only the first pressing, up to nearly 600 gallons of juice, may be made into champagne. The juice flows into large vats where the first fermentation, lasting up to six weeks, takes place. During the winter, the resulting wine is racked several times until it is clear. Then in spring this and other wines are blended together to make the *cuvée*, becoming a vintage *(millesimé)* if all are of the same year, non vintage · *(sans année)* if they are not.

The *dosage*, a measure of cane-sugar and pure yeast enzymes, is added to the wine before it is bottled. The bottles are then stacked *sur lattes* or on their sides in deep cellars. There they stay for three to five years, the enzymes transforming the sugar into alcohol and carbonic gas to make the wine effervescent. The first step in getting rid of the sediment formed by this secondary fermentation is to place the bottles *sur pointe* or neck down in wooden stands known as *pupitres*. Every day for several months the highly skilled *remuers* rotate the bottles, increasing the angle so that the sediment slides down to rest on the corks.

Next comes the *dégorgement*, which usually consists of freezing the necks of the bottles and removing the corks, when the sediment, imprisoned in a small block of ice, is shot out by the carbonic gas. The bottles are finally topped up with cane-sugar dissolved in mature champagne and Cognac. It is this that determines whether the wine will be dry, *demi-sec*, or sweet. The bottles are then sealed with new corks and the wine is left to settle. The quicker it is drunk after the *dégorgement* the better it will be.

There are different degrees of sparkle, from *cremant* and *petillant* to *mousseux*, just as there are different degrees of dryness. *Brut* means almost *nature*, *extra sec* is in fact a little less dry, *sec* is often more medium than dry, *demi-sec* is medium-sweet, and *doux* is sweet.

Blending has its virtues but the *dosage* can be overdone to cloak a mediocre wine and so demand is now growing for more natural champagnes, like the *millesimés*. The only drawback of these is their shorter life. The bigger the bottle, too, the longer lived the wine. Still in use in Champagne are the magnum, jeroboam, rehoboam, and mathusalem, holding the equivalent of two, four, six, and eight bottles. A good champagne does not go off with a bang when opened, nor does the wine froth out of the bottle. Champagne is usually regarded as a pre-meal drink. This is a role taken over in the region by *ratafia*, an aperitif of sweet champagne and locally made *marc* or fine Marne brandy. A dry champagne goes well with seasoned food, particularly freshwater fish; a *sec* or *demi-sec* with sweet dishes.

Much of the cuisine of Champagne is akin to ours, many of the dishes being delicately flavoured if somewhat heavy, though it includes a lot of rich game in season. A typical dish is larded chicken stuffed with onions, garlic, liver, and herbs, braised and then grilled. Another is *potée des vendangeurs*, a sort of *pot au feu* made with three or four kinds of meat and an even greater number of vegetables. Cabbage and potatoes are two vegetables as popular in Champagne as they are in Britain, though you might be less accustomed to *escargots* and salads made of *pissenlits* or dandelions.

Fish, like trout and pike, as well as crayfish, are often braised in *vin nature* or served with *beurre blanc*, a savoury sauce made with shallots, butter, and champagne. Some freshwater fish are cooked together in a wine-based *matelote*. Pork dishes are probably the most popular. They include stuffed pigs' trotters and the fine hams of Reims, often served *en croute* or encased in pastry. Also made of pork are the tasty chitterling sausages called *andouillettes* and the black-pudding kind known as *boudin*.

Champagne adjoins the Brie, famed for the flat round cheeses from its lush pastures. Those made in the region itself include tasty Boursault and the even stronger Maroilles. Sometimes served between courses is a *glacé au marc*, a 'water'-ice flavoured with brandy. An unusual pear grown around Reims is the *rousselet*, rich and juicy but unable to travel. Locally famed are the plump cherries of Dormans, beside the Marne. Melon is often marinaded in champagne before being served and the wine is used in the making of *sabayon*, which also contains egg yolks and sugar. Two specialities of Reims are flans made with Pinot Noir grapes and small macaroons, an enjoyable accompaniment to champagne.

In the wine villages and towns among the vineyards, restaurants are not as numerous as you might like but most of those that exist are small and homely. In any case, distances are short – the Côte des Blancs being a mere 13 miles long and the Montagne only 12 miles across in one direction and six in the other. Many of the champagne houses in Reims and Epernay close for the whole of August. It is only in these towns that parking can be difficult. The two roads carrying most traffic are the N51 linking Reims and Epernay and the N3 along the south bank of the Marne. Finding your way on the byways through the vineyards is made easier by the yellow Michelin map 56. On these roads, where to meet another car is an event, driving is relaxed and you have plenty of time to admire the views.

While it may be badly placed as a centre for touring the vineyards, Reims is nevertheless a good place from which to start. Well known for its

admirable Notre Dame Cathedral where most of the kings of France were crowned, the city is also one of the capitals of the wine trade (a role it shares with Epernay). The most animated part of Reims is the Place Drouet d'Erlon, west of the Cathedral.

The better-known champagne houses are grouped around the Champ de Mars on the north and near the basilica of St Remi on the south-east, neither district being far from the route taken by the busy N44 through the city. Best known of the first group are Lanson, Mumm, and Roederer; of the second, Veuve Clicquot, Taittinger, Ruinart, and Pommery and Greno. Greno has some impressive cellars incorporating galleries excavated by the Romans, their walls decorated with carvings cut in the chalk. Most of them are open daily and give guided tours, usually with English commentaries.

Leading south from Reims to Epernay, the N51 crosses the largely flat-topped Montagne de Reims rising up from the plain on either side. But here height is purely relative. Even if you take into account the *monts* of Sinai and Joli that dominate the eastern half of the plateau the altitude is nowhere more than 930ft. Crowning the Montagne is a vast beech forest inhabited by wild boar and deer. It is broken here and there by bare sandy wastes, and dry gulleys and springs where several subterranean rivers have their source. Crossing the N51 at Montchenot, a natural belvedere, is the winding and hilly road that loops round the plateau to link the wine villages and give changing views of the vineyards at nearly every turn.

West of Montchenot is Villedommange, with its fine 12th-century church in sight of the 15th-century pilgrimage Chapel of St Lie, built on a mound in the centre of a once-sacred wood. East of the N51, Rilly la Montagne is a handy centre for walks on Mont Joli, with its panoramic views of plateau and plain. A popular weekend trip for the people of Reims, Rilly is notable for its church incorporating sculptures relating to vines and wine. At nearby Ludes is an ancient Romanesque church and the *caves* or cellars of Canard Duchene, a *marque* of champagne better known in France than in England. A few miles north-east in the Vesle valley is Sillery, once well known for its single-growth wines.

All the vineyards in the commune of Mailly, east of Ludes, are in the *premier grand cru* category. In the depression of the Thirties, when the champagne houses did not have the money to pay an economic rate for the grapes, some 70 growers at Mailly decided to band together to make their own wine and store it until times improved. By doing so they have ensured that an earlier era of champagne has survived. The single-growth champagne of the Societé des Producteurs, as the growers' *co-operative* is called, is there-fore something special. Since it is from vineyards in the top category, it is probably unique among champagnes – bigger and more powerful than any blend and with a bouquet of new-mown hay. Something else that makes the *co-operative* special is its rosé. Usually, pink champagne is made by adding some still red wine of the region to the white before it is bottled for the secondary fermentation. But at Mailly they leave the skins of the Pinot Noir with the juice during the first fermentation, in the traditional way, which allows the must to take up the flavour and fullness of the grapes. The

7

The harvesting of grapes on behalf of the champagne house of Heidseck.

*co-operative* welcomes visitors to its cellars.

The picturesque village of Verzenay, a mile or two to the east, is also noted for its *premier grand cru* vineyards. On the outskirts is a windmill that was used as a vantage point in the 1914-18 war and is now owned by the champagne house of Heidseck. Ancient Verzy, on the eastern edge of the Montagne, grew up round the 7th-century Benedictine Abbey of St Basle, which like most others in France was destroyed during the Revolution. Near the ruined Abbey chapel off the D34 to the south-west are the Faux de Verzy, a group of grotesquely shaped beech trees five centuries old deformed by the high concentration of iron in the soil.

Most of the vineyards on the slopes of the Montagne face east, but those that stretch from nearby Ambonnay to Bouzy and beyond – all in the top category – have the advantage of facing south-east; one reason perhaps why they produce more delicate wines. From the pretty *village fleuri* of Ambonnay, the best way south is *par les vignes* to quaintly named Bouzy. Here, in good years, some of the vines produce a fragrant still red wine not unlike a Beaujolais. In the village are the cellars of Jean Paul Brice, a maker and champion of individual *crus* of champagne.

At nearby Tours sur Marne, built around an ancient priory, are the cellars of Laurent Perrier, the biggest producer of *vin nature* in the region. Champillon, beside the N51 on the southern slopes of the Montagne, has what is undoubtedly the best restaurant in the region, the Royal Champagne, housed in an ancient *relais de poste* which gives panoramic views of the vineyards.

West of Champillon is Hautvillers, a charming small town on a 1-in-7 slope with grandiose views of one of the most beautiful stretches of the Marne. Adjoining the ruined abbey where Dom Perignon studied ways to improve the wines of the region is the former abbey church containing his tomb.

Epernay, on the left bank of the Marne, is an attractive town of human scale and a convenient centre for touring the surrounding vineyards. Many of its streets are lined with classic façades, the most imposing being the Avenue de Champagne where many of the *grandes marques* have their headquarters. Most of these buildings, elaborately decorated, date like the cellars beneath them from the 18th century. Most welcoming are Moet et Chandon, Mercier (with over ten miles of cellars which visitors tour by train), and Perrier Jouet. Château Perrier in the same street houses the museum of Champagne, made up of many fascinating exhibits and audio-visual aids. Near by, in the Rue Henri-Lelarge, are the premises of Pol Roger where vast cellars house what was once Winston Churchill's favourite drink.

From Epernay it is a beautiful drive across the winding Marne and through the south-facing vineyards extending east and west along the opposite bank, known locally as la Rivière. Most of the vineyards were originally planted on estates owned by the bishops of Reims in Carolingian times.

Facing Epernay across the Marne is Ay (pronounced Ai-ee), backed by its celebrated vineyard dating from Gallo-Roman days. In one of the town's winding streets, lined with winegrowers' houses enclosing internal court-yards, is a half-timbered building said to have been the *vendangeoir* of the jolly Gascon, Henri IV. The small cemetery set in the vineyard on the outskirts of the town occupies some of the most expensive land in the world. Ay wines are of great renown and possess perfect balance of body and delicacy. A little-publicised but *grande marque* all the same is Deutz, founded at Ay in 1838. It was tagged with its German name during the Napoleonic era when France established an *entente cordiale* with the Palatinate across the Rhine and many dynamic young Germans arrived in Champagne to learn the wine trade. A number of them, apprenticed to *négociants,* eventually married the daughters of their otherwise heirless employers and took over the businesses. A better-known *négociant* at Ay is Bollinger, which makes its champagne in the old fashioned way – fruity yet full flavoured.

Along with Ay, nearby Mareuil claims to produce the best wine of the Rivière. Near the village is the 18th-century château bought in 1830 by the Duke of Montebello, one of Napoleon's officers better known as Marshal Lannes, which is now the headquarters of the champagne house of the same

9

name. Downstream is Cumières, from which a picturesque road leads to Hautvillers, and Damery, a popular spot for fishing and bathing in the Marne and still with its old quays dating from the time when it was an active river port.

Over to the west, Chatillon, with a ruined feudal castle and fine riverscapes, was the birthplace of Pope Urban II, preacher of the first Crusade in 1095. Beyond more vineyards terraced above the river is the small town of Dormans, damaged in several recent wars, where a chapel commemorates the two battles of the Marne in 1914 and 1918. Close by is an ancient church and a château of the Louis XIII period.

Epernay is also a handy base for drives south along the ridge called the Côte des Blancs astride the N51. It gets its name not from the colour of the soil but because its eastern slopes are planted mainly with Chardonnay vines bearing white grapes. The soft and delicate wines these produce are an essential element in brand-name blends, though as Blanc de Blancs they also make wines in their own right. A rare Blanc de Noirs is made, too. Except for the woods crowning the summit of the crest it is entirely covered with vines. At its foot are the slate-roofed villages of the *vignerons,* their winding and narrow streets bordered by great double doors opening into wide courtyards.

In the green Cubry valley west of the N51 are the peaceful villages of Vinay and St Martin d'Ablois, but the major part of the Côte is to the east of the main road. On the heights, a short way beyond the pleasant village of Cramant, is Avize, with a school for winegrowers and an interesting part-Romanesque church. Cramant and Avize are two of the top 12 *premiers grands crus* in Champagne.

Next comes Oger and its irregularly shaped twin le Mensnil sur Oger, and, a few miles on, Vertus, backed by 1,200 acres of vines, half of them planted with Pinot Noir, from which come rounded and full-bodied wines of astonishing quality. Centred on natural springs called Les Puits St Martin, Vertus was once a lively market town but now lives solely by wine, the line of its former ramparts traced by a ring of boulevards.

Marking the southern limit of the Côte des Blancs is the 770ft-high isolated hill of Mount Aimé adjoining Bergeres les Vertus, occupied since prehistoric times and fortified and tunnelled in turn by Gauls and Romans. The hill is topped by the crumbling ruins of the Château de la Reine Blanche, built by the counts of Champagne in feudal times. From the orientation table near the ruins, the view extends for miles across the chalk plain on one side and the marshes on the other.

Anyone who explores the vineyards from which the unique and world-famous champagne comes might well agree that their setting has all the grace and freshness of the wine itself.

# Alsace

The charm of Alsace is concentrated in its picturesque wine villages and towns: in their winding streets decorated by fountains, in their half-timbered houses weighed down by red-tiled roofs, and in their church spires and chimneys crowned by storks' nests. Strung out on a line north and south of Colmar and bordered on the east by the fertile Rhine plain, the vineyard area enclosing them is dominated to the west by the green and friendly Vosges mountains that ward off cold winds and rain clouds to make it one of the sunniest and driest parts of France. The landscape is charming, too, still abounding in the 'pleasant views and inequalities' noted by the Suffolk squire Arthur Young when he passed this way in 1788.

Along with the rest of Alsace the region has been the shuttlecock of history: French from 1678, German from 1871, French again in 1918, German a second time in 1940, and, finally, French once more in 1945. Perhaps it is as a result of this that the wine villages and towns have a German flavour, but their inhabitants, proud as they may be of their separate identity, are essentially French. Not that the conservative Alsatians would give up what they call their language, any more than they would their ancient traditions or their folklore. Still, their *patois* puts up no great obstacles to the stranger as most locals speak either English or French. Probably its only drawback are the tongue-twisting names it gives to the villages and towns.

Pronouncing the names of the wines is easier, though, as Alsace has a tradition of marketing them by the name of the grape from which they are made, the vineyard or village only now beginning to be mentioned on the label.

This is predominantly white wine country. Mostly drunk young, the natural and straightforward wines even when full bodied have a grapey flavour and bouquet and give an impression of lightness, striking a happy balance between alcohol, acidity, and fruitiness. This gives the better vintages a freshness that can be retained in bottle for 6 to 15 years or more. These are some of the cleanest, most honest wines made anywhere.

The first group are what the Alsatians call *vins de table* or wines for everyday drinking with food. Chasselas (or Gutedel) is light, fresh, and not too dry. It forms the bulk of the carafe wine served in local bars by the glass or on the terraces of cafés and homely *auberges* in earthenware jugs in summer. A related hybrid is Knipperlé. Zwicker is a blend of *vins fins* or fine wines and no less agreeable for that. Edelzwicker is a superior blend, usually of Sylvaner and Pinot Blanc; *edel* in this context means 'noble'. Made from a middle-quality grape, Sylvaner is a soft and fruity wine, often elegant, and ready to drink a few months after the vintage. When grown in the soil that suits it, as around Colmar, it can be excellent. Lighter but equally fruity, Pinot is well balanced. A few light refreshing red wines made from Pinot Noir are served chilled like the whites.

The *vins nobles* or quality wines begin with Muscat, often served as an aperitif, exceptionally dry, light, and with a big grapey bouquet. Enhanced by the alcohol, the bouquet and flavour are even more pronounced than the newly gathered grapes themselves. The driest of all Alsatian wines (the only one of its kind in France), it is a far cry from the cloying dessert wines made from the same grape elsewhere. The 'true aristocrat of Alsace' is the Riesling, a well-known vine variety introduced from Germany. Lively and exquisitely fruity, it has a bouquet as clear as a bell and a flavour in the mouth that is fresh and elegant. The vine is prolific elsewhere but here it is a light cropper and does not stand up to frost or wet weather. Tokay (or Pinot Gris) is an opulent wine, full bodied, high in acidity, and strong. Last on the list are the twins Gewurztraminer and Traminer. Spicy, full bodied, and often heady, they have a perfume and flavour so concentrated that they often give a false impression of sweetness. Gewurztraminer clearly owes its name to the practice in ancient times of adding spice – in German, *gewurz* – to wine to cover up its earthy taste, a habit unnecessarily carried on by present-day makers of mulled wine and punch. Gewurztraminer usually needs to be aged for three years in bottle before drinking, so those dated 1971 – an exceptional year for all Alsace wines – should be close to their peak. Some growers maintain that 1973 was even better.

Cloaking the eastern foothills of the Vosges, the splendid vineyards are good to look at and, being in full sun from daybreak onwards, pleasant to wander among. Though devastated by numerous wars, they still make up the highest density of small vineyards in France. It was the great religious orders which developed the original vineyards – from the 8th century onwards catering not only for their own needs but also getting most of their revenue from the wines. As in other parts of France, it was the English who from the 13th century took the bulk of the wines and by the 14th century, when the Rhine was even then the most important waterway in Europe, the vineyards covered an area half as big again as it is now. Later on, the weakness of the German empire (of which Alsace was then a part) allowed the creation of customs barriers to hamper the wine trade: on the Rhine between Cologne and Strasbourg there were no less than 53. With the Germans who occupied Alsace in 1870 came phylloxera and mildew to destroy the vines. From then until 1918, Alsace, like its wines, sank into oblivion. Only now are the growers able to maintain their former high standards and only now are the wines becoming as well known as they were in the Middle Ages.

Left to themselves, Alsatian growers may be sticklers for tradition but they are also open to new ideas: the differing colours of the strips of paper fluttering over the vineyards act as a guide to the pilot of the aircraft about to spray them with copper sulphate. They cover 25,000 acres and if demand for the wines justified it, they could be increased by a third as much again. But anyone thinking of buying a vineyard in Alsace needs to be prepared to pay dearly for it – anything from £12,000 to £30,000 an acre.

The grape harvest goes on until the end of October, picking starting on the lower slopes where the best vineyards are and working upwards. All vineyards except those of the *co-operatives* are family owned. One in five growers makes his own wine, leaving it to mature in oak casks for up to six months. The *co-operatives* join together as many as 4,000 growers and make up a third of the total production of 100 million bottles a year.

Alsace was the last region to win an *appellation controlée* for its wines, though now over two thirds of them qualify for it. All the wines are bottled — mostly by the growers themselves – in the traditional long green *flute*.

Alsatian cuisine is as original as the wines and its richness is in turn balanced by the lightness of the wines. Backed by well-stocked larders, Alsatians are solid eaters; yet they also like the 'spice' of such things as pieces of Munster cheese dipped in caraway seed.

Soup is the usual starter to a meal; the most popular one is not unexpectedly based on frogs' legs. There are over 40 different pâtés, some served hot, most prized of which is of course the costly *foie gras* or goose liver. Nowhere is cooked pig held in higher esteem: as well as sucking pig and *jambon en croute* appearing on menus, the range of pork meats (including sausages of varying shapes and tastes) is extensive. Rhine salmon is now only a memory but from the streams of the Vosges come trout and the pike, carp, tench, perch, and eel that go into the popular wine-based *matelote*.

Cabbages of enormous size are grown in the fertile Rhine plain for shredding and fermenting in barrels to make *choucroute*. This must traditionally be prepared with goose fat, remain white, and still have 'bite' to it when cooked – retaining the acidity of the fermentation and the white wine. Served garnished with sausage, pork, ham, and bacon (or on occasion wildfowl or pheasant), it is the traditional dish around which all others revolve.

The fine chickens are often cooked in wine as *coq au riesling* and the savoury flesh of geese is sometimes enhanced by being smoked, as in *poitrine d'oie fumée*. Two dishes of ancient origin are *baeckeoffe* (or *beckenoffe*), a casserole of mutton, beef, pork, and vegetables, and stuffed breast of veal. This is one of the best parts of France for game. Fine orchard fruits go into mouth-watering *tartes* or flans. The soft and strong Munster cheese from the valley of the same name adjoining the vineyards appears almost everywhere, and every *patisserie* has a display of the traditional *kugelhopf* cakes.

To round off a meal there are many fine *eaux de vie*, most of them made from fruit – though they are not at all the same thing as liqueurs. Dry to the taste and as clear as water, they range from *kirsch* or cherry through *sureau* (elderberry), *myrtille* (bilberry), and *mure* (mulberry) to *quetsche* or plum. *Marc de gewurtztraminer*, usually served with a lump of sugar, is even more powerfully perfumed than the wine from the grape itself.

The suggested route through the vineyards follows for much of the way the signposted *route du vin*, which winds its leisurely way through the wine villages and towns for a distance of 70-odd miles. Not a long way to drive, perhaps, but needing at least a week if you are to make the most of it. Many of the small towns in the vineyards – where most of the hotels are quaintly ancient rather than luxurious – are floodlit in summer. The region is covered by the yellow Michelin map 87.

Attempt to describe the charm of the wine villages and small towns of Alsace and you will soon run out of superlatives. Northernmost of these is Marlenheim, on the busy N4 linking Nancy and Strasbourg. Here, there are some excellent restaurants specialising in traditional regional dishes, and

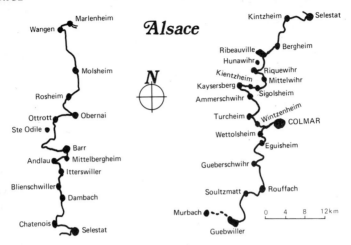

there are several old coaching inns, of which the Cerf is probably the best example. The only 'dry' day for people wanting to taste the wines from the nearby vineyards is Friday: Jerome Fritsch caters for them at weekends, Clement Fend on Mondays and Tuesdays, and Michel Laugen on Wednesdays and Thursdays.

From Marlenheim the *route du vin* (N422) leads south to Wangen, which holds its Fête de la Fontaine on the Sunday following 3 July, when the water that normally flows from the fountain at the heart of its winding streets is replaced by wine as a reminder of the time when the villagers had to pay a tithe of 300 hectolitres of the annual vintage to the local lord.

A short way on, the small medieval town of Molsheim nestles within its ruined ramparts at the foot of the Molsheimer Berg, cloaked in vines and crowned by an ancient fortress. At its centre is a triangular *place* bordered by 16th-17th-century half-timbered houses and overlooked by the handsome Renaissance-style Metzig, built in 1528 for the local butchers' guild. The upper floor is reached by a fine external staircase. The ground floor, occupied by the *caveau* run by the municipality, is where the wines from the Berg can be sampled. A modest wine fair is held in the town on the first Thursday in May. Founded in 1618, the church is relatively recent – it once belonged to the famous Jesuit academy – but on the outskirts is the Dompeter, the oldest church in Alsace.

On its way south, the wine road leaves the *route nationale* to turn west towards the Vosges and reach Rosheim, an anciently fortified small town. In one of the streets is the 12th-century Heidenhaus, the oldest house for miles around. Other venerable structures are the three fortified gates, the 12th-century Peter and Paul Church, and several ornately decorated wells and fountains. In the Rue Clemenceau are the premises of two wine growers who welcome visitors, Ingert-Koenig and Xavier Klein.

Near by is the delightful and typically Alsatian town of Obernai, dominated on the west by Mont Ste Odile. A statue of the Saint stands close by a Renaissance fountain in the central Place de la Mairie, bordered on one side by the wide-gabled Halle aux Blés or corn market built in 1554 (housing a popular *brasserie* and an interesting museum of local life) and on the other by the town hall erected 31 years before. In the streets leading off the square are many old half-timbered houses, their high roofs decorated with tiles of contrasting colours, their wooden balconies brimming over with geraniums and other flowers. The dry climate of Alsace suits not only vines but tobacco plants as well and in October many of the hotel rooms are taken by the men from the state monopoly who come to assess the crop. Unhappily their arrival coincides with the vintage festival, held on the second Sunday of the same month, when gaily decorated floats rumble through the cobbled streets and the town-hall square is decked with garlands and filled, or so it seems, with casks from which girls in traditional costume serve the heady *vin nouveau* to all comers.

West of Obernai is Ottrot, one of the few places in Alsace producing rosé and red wines as well as white – in the Rue du Château leading west to the ruined castle above the village are the cellars of Eugene Schaetzel where some of them can be sampled. In season a narrow-gauge tourist-train operates between Ottrot and Rosheim, to the north.

The high spur of the nearby Vosges is Mont Ste Odile. Whilst famed for its views, it is more important to the people of Alsace for its associations with their patron saint, Odile. Her tomb – housed in a 12th-century chapel – is the goal of many pilgrimages during the year, the most important being on Easter Monday. The nuns of the convent still give food and drink to the pilgrims, as others before them have done for centuries. Beyond Heiligenstein, with the ruined Château of Landsberg towering above, is the delightful small town and important wine centre of Barr. Its narrow streets and squares lined by half-timbered houses are centred on the castle built in 1640 where the annual *foire aux vins* or wine fair is held on the last Thursday in March. The town is even gayer during its wine festival on the first Sunday in October. The vines on the nearby slopes produce mostly Sylvaner and Gewurtztraminer. The two Klipfel brothers, Louis and Eugene, are glad to give visitors a taste of them at their separate premises in the Avenue de la Gare.

There are also plenty of places to sample wines in the neighbouring village of Mittelbergheim. In the verdant valley of the same name is Andlau, backed on the north by a ruined 14th-century château. Quaint old houses enclose the 12th-century abbey church, with its portal decorated by remarkable Romanesque sculpture.

The way south passes through Itterswiller and Blienschwiller to the pretty *village fleuri* with the rather grand name – notwithstanding its population of 2,000 – of Dambach la Ville. Justification for its title of 'town' comes from the combination of its medieval ramparts, three fortified gates flanked by big towers, its 16th-century town hall, the Chapel of St Sebastien, the sandstone castle of Bernstein, and the dozen growers' cellars that line the streets.

Near the junction of two rivers flowing down from the Vosges, Chatenois has a church with a curious belfry and a 15th-century gateway called the Tour des Sorcieres (Sorcerers) – topped some summers by nesting storks.

To the east, in the rich plain of Alsace, is ancient Selestat, once a flourishing university city – which explains why the *bibliothèque* contains the entire library of Beatus Rhenanus and other valuable manuscripts. Although the town is now partly industrialized, it still preserves its old quarter beside the river Ill and is still concerned with wine. Starting on the first Sunday in August, its combined wine fair and festival lasts the whole week.

West of Selestat one rejoins the *route du vin* at Kintzheim, where in the grounds of the château off the Haut Koenigsbourg road a flight of eagles demonstrate their prowess at hunting vipers and other prey – but only on dry days, apparently, for it seems that this is one species of bird unable to fly when its wing feathers are wet. The road continues through Orschwiller to St Hippolyte, noted for the number of fountains in its streets and squares and for its red and more plentiful white wines.

Rebuilt after the fierce fighting that went on around it in the Colmar 'pocket' in 1944, Bergheim, a short way south, is another of the half-dozen places in Alsace producing a red wine from Pinot Noir vines. At the heart of the vineyards is a homely *auberge* and not far away, in the Rue des Vignerons, are the *caveaux* of Gustave Lorentz and Jules Muller. Typically, these are also their family homes handed down like their vineyards from father to son. The main artery of nearby Ribeauvillé, in a romantic setting at the foot of the Vosges overlooked by the ruined castles of Girsberg, St Ulrich, and Rappolstein, is the cobbled Grande Rue bordered by ancient half-timbered houses, the Trois Rois Inn (a haven for travellers since 1540), the fortified Tour des Bouchers gate, and the church of the convent of the hermits of St Augustine, dating from 1412. Noted for its Traminer and Riesling wines, the town is also famous as the meeting place in times past of the wandering minstrels of the Rhine, who gathered here on Pfiffertag or fife day every year to pay homage to their protectors, the local lords. The tradition is kept alive by the annual fête held on the first Sunday in September, when free wine flows from the Renaissance fountain in the town hall square.

Wines from the vineyards climbing the slopes on the west are shown at a modest *foire aux vins* in Ribeauvillé on the first Tuesday in May. Those made by Louis Sipp can be tasted at his cellars in the Grand Rue at the usual times, those of the *co-operative vinicole* at the Zahnacker restaurant on the *route du vin* at almost any hour of the day or night. But anyone interested in superbly cooked food served in idyllic surroundings should drive the five miles east to Illhaeusern and the Auberge de l'Ill, one of the twelve best restaurants in France, where goose liver encased in pastry and salmon soufflé often feature on the lengthy menu.

Another detour worth making is to the village of Hunawihr. Here, there is a welcoming *co-operative vinicole,* a fountain dedicated to its patron Huna from which wine is said to gush forth whenever the grape harvest is bad, and a 16th-century church isolated in the vineyards. The hexagonal fortifications that ring the church incorporate a sentry port at each angle and its belfry, built like a castle keep, adds a second line of defence. Hunawihr holds its *kilbe* or village fête in mid July. The wine you should ask to sample at the *co-operative* is the infrequently found red.

The 'pearl of the Alsatian vineyards' is undoubtedly Riquewihr, to the south, a charming small town which happily emerged unscathed from the last war and so perpetuates the Middle Ages in both plan and elevation. Within the ramparts is a veritable open-air museum: an antique church for Protestants, another for Catholics, ancient fortified gates, ornate wells and fountains, 15th-century houses with sculptured doorways, flower-decked balconies and enclosed courtyards, and wrought-iron signs and carved inscriptions. Among the quaint old inns in the Grande Rue, their interiors darkened by blackened oak beams, is the venerable Cerf dating from 1566. The Tour des Voleurs was once a prison and of course incorporates the obligatory torture chamber. The Dolder or High Gate houses a small museum illustrating life in Riquewihr through the ages.

Best known of the growers offering tastings of their wines is the Hugel family, twelve generations of whom have been making wine in the town for over 300 years. In their cellars (closed for the second half of August) is the huge Catherine fermenting vat, made of stout oak in 1715 and holding 8,800 litres, said to be the oldest still in use. Two other establishments with familiar names are Dopff et Irion and Preiss Zimmer.

Special characteristics of the local subsoil and the growers' know-how apart, the high quality of the wines is largely due to the vineyards that encircle the town – the planting of inferior vine varieties has been banned there since 1595. Beyond the famous named vineyard of Sonnenglanz (Sunshine) at Beblenheim is the village of Mittelwihr, noted for its fine Riesling and Gewurztraminer wines, where the vineyards are so well exposed to the sun that the district is called the Midi of Alsace. Even the almond trees bear fruit. At the southern edge of the village, rebuilt after being badly damaged in the last war, is the wall of the 'martyred flowers', in

Riquewihr: 'pearl of the Alsatian vineyards'.

Almost an aerial view of Riquewihr – from the top of the vineyard.

front of which (during the German occupation) the villagers planted blue pansies, white petunias, and red geraniums to represent the French tricolour. Worth a call at the adjoining village of Bennwihr is the biggest *co-operative* in Alsace.

From the *village fleuri* of Sigolsheim, dating from Merovingian times, and the burial place of 1,500 French soldiers killed during the fighting of 1944-45, the route turns west to follow the Weiss river and enter the ramparts of Kientzheim through the Porte Basse. This is a fortified gate topped by a sculptured head scowling towards Sigolsheim, perpetuating in stone the dislike the two villages once had for each other. In the church is the tomb of Lazare de Schwendi, the local bailiff who in the 16th century is said to have brought back the first Tokay vines from the village of that name in Hungary.

Surrounded by fine vineyards in a pretty situation at the opening of the Weiss valley is the small town of Kaysersberg, named after Caesaris Mons, a Roman fort that commanded the important route between eastern Gaul and the Rhine. The main sights are the ruined château, the fortified 16th-century bridge across the river, and the house where the scientist and son of the local pastor Albert Schweitzer was born in 1875. Combining tastings of the new wine with folklore events, the vintage festival takes place in late September or early October.

South-east, at the foot of slopes inset with the named vineyard of Kaefferkopf, Ammerschwihr lost many of its ancient buildings during the battle for the Colmar 'pocket' in December 1944 and January 1945 – although the deep wine cellars beneath the houses saved many a life by being used as shelters. The Kuehn *caveau* in the Grande Rue is only one of the various places where visitors can try the wines. Alsatians have long believed that storks are a sign of good luck. Each spring they wait for the birds to arrive, often erecting platforms on their roofs to encourage them to settle there and build their heavy nests. After a couple of months the young are able to fly and in August (under a parental wing) they set off on the traditional route across France and Spain to winter like idle rich in southern Africa. But storks feed on fish and as more of the marshes along the Rhine are drained fewer and fewer of them return to Alsace.

One of three fortified gates set in the triangular-shaped ramparts of the delightful small town of Turckheim near by is the 14th-century Porte de France topped by a specially constructed platform on which, if the towns-folk are lucky, a pair of storks have built their nest. (True aristocrats, these birds will only settle on the highest point in a village or town.) The last place in Europe to have kept its *nachtwachter* or night watchman, who makes his rounds each evening calling out the hours, Turckheim is also famous as the location of the Brand vineyard. The wines from this and other vineyards – including a red from Pinot Noir – can be sampled at the Caveau des Vignerons in the Grande Rue, bordered by quaint old houses, or in the beautifully decorated 17th-century Deux Clefs Inn near by.

South of Turckheim, on the far side of the river Fecht, is Wintzenheim, on the main road linking Colmar with one of the most attractive parts of the Vosges. Hansel and Gretel architecture abounds in the beautiful old heart of Colmar, its squares decorated with fountains and its streets overhung by tall timber-framed and gabled houses, their roofs decorated with coloured tiles arranged in lozenge patterns, their fronts hung with wrought-iron signs and ornamented with curious carvings. Each upper floor was corbelled out in medieval times to obtain more space without having to buy more land, always costly in Alsace. In those days, too, the exposed beams on the façades were protected by daubing them with a mixture of ox blood and herbs.

The most important building in the *centre ville* is the Unterlinden Museum containing the famous Issenheim altarpiece painted by Mathias Grunwald of Franconia in the 16th century. The monastic Order of Issenheim was founded in 1090 to care for the victims of a skin infection called St Anthony's fire, and the painting is a powerful blend of realism and mysticism. Other notable buildings in Colmar are the Ancienne Douane, the Maison Pfister, and the medieval guardhouse, not to mention the severely styled station built of red sandstone from the Vosges by the occupying Germans in 1905.

Colmar has been the centre of the Alsatian wine trade for centuries and at the fair staged in mid August the wines are grouped together, with all the Rieslings on one stand, all the Sylvaners on another, and so on. Growers add their labelled and numbered bottles to each group, making it easy for the taster to compare wines from the same grape – although produced by a dozen or more vineyards – to remember the one he liked best, then look for the grower's name among the Muscats to see how he has done there. The atmosphere is an enjoyable combination of good cheer and genuine interest in the wines.

At other times the wines can be sampled at the Bourse aux Vins in the Rue des Têtes or at the premises of individual growers like Jacobert, who not only offers a *degustation* of his wines but of the *eaux de vie blanches* he makes as well. And in the narrow streets there are many modest *winstubs* where you can wash down the local specialities with a carafe of honest *ordinaire*. The way south from Colmar passes through Wettolsheim, where the Romans are said to have planted the first vines in Alsace. Beyond is Eguisheim, a picturesque and typically Alsatian village which – like the way of life of the people living there – remains much as it was in the 16th century. Dominating the skyline on the south-west are the sandstone keeps of three ruined castles. Several houses in the Rue du Rempart Sud, their big double doors opening into internal courtyards, remain forlornly empty – however inexpensive to buy, they are too costly to modernise, at least within the framework of the strictly enforced regulations designed to preserve the façades.

The *co-operative vinicole* of Eguisheim, one of the biggest in Alsace, welcomes visitors at its premises in the Grande Rue and at the Caveau restaurant one can savour the wines along with traditional Alsatian food. One wine produced by the *co-operative*, rarely met with outside the region, is the *petillant* or sparkling Blanc de Blancs.

Near by is Husseren les Châteaux, the suffix referring to the three ruined castles of Eguisheim west of the village. Husseren has the highest altitude vineyards in Alsace (1,300ft), some of which are owned by Arthur Schueller whose *cave* is near the church.

The byway passing through the pretty village of Gueberschwihr, dominated by a fine 12th-century belfry, joins the main N83 on its way south to the ancient and prosperous agricultural town of Rouffach. Here, there is a picturesque old quarter around the main square overlooked by a 16th-century town hall and a crenellated sorcerer's tower of the 13th century. Interesting statues and tombs line the walls of the nearby 13th-century Franciscan church, topped in good years by a stork's nest.

Reached by a road running west from Rouffach is the charming small town of Soultzmatt extended along the banks of the Ohmbach river, as well known for its mineral water as for its wines. To the south is Bergholtzell, with an 11th-century church consecrated by Pope Leo IX, born at Eguisheim in 1002, two years after the date when medieval people thought the world might end.

A tourist resort and a market for local wines, the medium-size town of Guebwiller stands at the point where the pretty Lauch valley opens out at the foot of the Vosges. In the town is the *caveau* of Schlumberger, the owner of extensive vineyards, a museum devoted to life in the Lauch valley (known as the Florival or valley of flowers), numerous old houses, and several interesting churches. Dominating the view to the south-west is the rounded summit of the Grand Ballon, at 4,620ft the highest point of the Vosges.

Off the road north-west out of the town, that follows the Lauch upstream into the Vosges, is a byway leading to the celebrated Abbey of Murbach, founded in 727, whose prince-abbot – answering only to the pope and the emperor – ruled religious life in Guebwiller and the surrounding district with an iron hand for centuries. All that remains of the Abbey now is the twin-towered church, rebuilt in red sandstone in 1175. In the south crossing of the transept is the tomb of Eberhard of Eguisheim, protector of the Order.

# Jura

The Jura's antique vineyards, extending in a narrow band rarely more than three miles wide along the superbly scenic slopes of the Jura plateau, are the only ones in the world to produce five distinct types of wine. From north to south the main growths – all covered by *appellations d'origine contrôlées* – are Arbois, the legendary Château Chalon, Etoile, and Côtes du Jura. The climate is semi-continental: warm and dry in summer and autumn, hard in winter. Many of the vines are planted on steep terraces, to which the earth washed down by the winter rains has to be carried back up each spring.

This is one of the few wine-growing areas of France where rosés take pride of place over red wines. Poulsard (or Ploussard) and Trousseau, the traditional vines of Arbois and its neighbouring communes, have less colouring in their skins than most other black-grape varieties. Rosé is usually made by leaving juice and skins together for no longer than is necessary to give the wine the right amount of colour. In the Jura they may ferment together for days, as they would for red wine, and yet the resultant hue is still never deeper than a strong pink. It is this extended *cuvage* which gives the Jura rosé its body, flavour, and the staying power of red wine.

The red wine, fresh and fruity when young and often made by fermenting Poulsard alone or with Trousseau and Pinot Noir together, takes on the colour of *pelure d'oignon*, or onion skin, with age – at the same time as it develops a more delicate bouquet. In good years it is aged for three years in oak casks before being bottled.

The white wines of this region have a remarkable bouquet. Though it has affinities with the Traminer of the Rhine, the late ripening Savagnin is said to have developed from Tokay vines brought back from Hungary in the 12th century by Jean I, Lord of Chalon. From it comes the unique *vin jaune*, mostly from the commune of Château Chalon but also from Arbois. Except that the grapes are often harvested as late as mid November, it begins life as an ordinary white wine. Once fermented, it is racked into casks where it remains for a minimum of six years. The bungs are loosened and despite steady evaporation, the barrels are never topped up. A film gradually spreads over the surface – as on sherry – and works on the wine below, deepening its colour to a rich amber and infusing it with the austere flavour of the *jaune*. When ready, it is bottled in traditional wide-shouldered *clavelins*, in which it keeps indefinitely.

Whatever some local restaurateurs may say, *vin jaune* does not lend itself to drinking throughout a meal. It is not really a table wine at all. The best way to drink it is chilled as an apéritif or at room temperature with the Comté cheese of the region.

*Vin de paille* is something else again. The grapes, from a judicious amalgamation of Poulsard, Trousseau, Chardonnay, and Savagnin vines, are gathered and placed on straw (hence the name) or hung up to dry for three months or more. When pressed and fermented they produce a sweet and strong white wine containing up to 16° of alcohol. Its price results from taking 200 lb of grapes and a great deal of time and trouble to produce every 18 litres of wine. The wine, which should be served lightly chilled, has a life in bottle of 100 years or more.

Sparkling wines have been produced in the Jura for over a century. The best, which go well with desserts, are those of Etoile (white), Arbois, and Côtes du Jura (white and rosé). The Chardonnay, called the melon in the northern Jura and Gamay Blanc in the south, lends itself when mixed with Pinot Noir to the making of a light and fruity *vin mousseux* by the *méthode champenoise*, involving a secondary fermentation in bottle of nine months. Covered by the yellow Michelin map 70, the 'wine road' of the Jura gives those who travel along it close-up views of some of the most magnificent mountain scenery in France, particularly where the rim of the plateau is notched by *reculées* or deep valleys crowned by high limestone cliffs. Admittedly some of the byways it follows are narrow, but since the route mostly skirts the western edge of the plateau motoring is never difficult. Finding somewhere to stay and eat along it poses no problems, either, for it is strung with wayside *auberges* and homely hotels where the food is invariably good and, as one would have every reason to expect in an area as unspoiled as this, the nights are peaceful.

Living as they do in a region abundant in lush pastures, dense pine forests, serried orchards, and rushing streams and rivers, the people of the Jura have always eaten well, whatever the hard times endured elsewhere. From the pastures come fine beef and creamy milk made into delicious butter and tangy cheeses, from the forests tasty *morilles* (a species of mushroom) and a variety of game, and from the orchards succulent plums, pears, and cherries. The rivers and streams are stocked with any number of 'main course' fish: these include trout and young pike (often baked as *brocheton au four*), perch and carp likely to eventually be cooked in white wine as a *pauchouse*, and crayfish which provide the basis of the famous speciality of *gratin*. Here, *quenelles* of flaked pike are more likely to be 'home made' rather than industrialized as they often are elsewhere. Game from the forests includes pheasant and woodcock, jugged hare in Arbois wine called *chaudronnée de lievre*, venison, and *marcassin* or wild boar. Chicken is prepared with cream or more expensively with the famous wine as *coq au vin jaune*. The range of pork meats or *charcuterie* is extensive, from *boudin* and *andouillette* sausages served hot to smoked varieties served cold along with raw smoked-ham and *porc en gelée*. Pâtés made of game and more conventional ingredients appear on most menus, but a dish not likely to be found in restaurants is *gaude* or boiled maize, eaten as a savoury or a sweet; with vegetables and beef it forms the basis of the popular *potée*, a rich soup. As well as the gruyère cheese usually referred to as *comté*, made throughout the Jura, there are blue-veined ones and the soft and mild *vacherin*.

Here, where it is traditional to drink the wine of the year – only one glass at a time, according to the local adage – there are numerous *digestifs* to ease the discomfort that follows eating not wisely but too well. Among the fruit brandies are *mirabelle* (yellow plum), *prunelle* (sloe), and *kirsch* (cherry). Another after-meal drink is *liqueur de sapin*, which tastes not unlike what the doctor ordered but is equally effective.

Northern gateway to the vineyard area, traversed by the main Besançon-Bourg en Bresse road N83, is the pleasant village of Port Lesney. In a charming setting of woods and water on the left bank of the Loue, it is popular at weekends with canoeists and anglers. Notable sights are the ruined 15th-century château on a rocky spur, the towers of an ancient abbey, and the 18th-century Chapel of Notre Dame de Lorette. The walks along the river are delightful.

South-east of Mouchard, with its national forestry school, is the ancient fortified town of Salins-les-Bains strung out along the narrow and picturesque valley of the Furieuse, flanked on the west by the Fort-St-André and on the east by the Fort-du-Haut-Belin, both built by Louis XIV's military architect Vauban. Most important thermal spa of the Jura and one of the oldest in France, complete with casino, it gets its name from the *salines* or salt springs discovered there over 2,000 years ago. In the early Middle Ages a *saline* was as valuable as a gold mine and anyone caught stealing salt was summarily hanged. The underground galleries leading to the *salines* are open to visitors, the 12th-century St Anatoile Church has a finely carved door and portal, and there are pleasant walks along the Promenade des Cordeliers above the Furieuse – an apt name for the river during the spring thaws. The two Vauban forts make an interesting excursion, too. Salins is noted for the white *vin mousseux* that comes from the Pinot Blanc vineyards surrounding the town.

South of Mouchard near the more direct route south is Les Arsures, a hamlet that prides itself on its red wine. In a setting of 'hanging woods and golden glens', the attractive small town of Arbois a few miles on is dominated by the high-domed belfry of its 13th-century church, bisected by the pretty river Cuisance, spanned by the ancient Pont des Capucins, and decked with vineyards on either bank. Home town of Pasteur, this is also the headquarters of Henri Maire, biggest wine producer in the Jura and *vigneron de père en fils* for over 300 years, whose answer to American cola

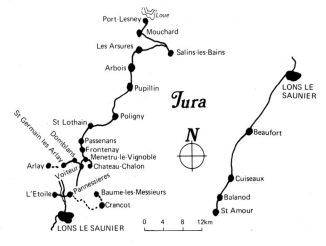

drinks is the sparkling Vin Fou, advertised it seems along every main road in France. But this is only one of a vast range of Henri Maire wines from vine-yards scattered throughout the region, many of which can be sampled at Les Deux Tonneaux in the centre of the town. Here, callers may be invited to drink from a *trinquette* – a cornet-shaped goblet of Merovingian origin without a stem or a foot which, since it cannot be put down, is more likely to be frequently topped up.

Henri Maire's grandfather was a friend of Pasteur, who in 1874 bought a small vineyard at Les Rosières (at the junction of the Besançon and Montigny les Arsures roads to the north of Arbois), where he conducted his experiments into fermentation and the other aspects of wine reported in his *Etudes sur le Vin*. Like the house beside the Cuisance where the great scientist spent his early life, the vineyard still exists, though the Friends of Pasteur have entrusted it to Henri Maire and the wine from it is reserved for special occasions. Arbois wines can also be tasted at the wine *co-operative* in the Place de la Liberté, called like others in the Jura *fruitière vinicole*, the word *fruitière* being borrowed from the joint enterprise dairies unique to the region. The white wines of the *co-operative* go down well with many of the specialities served at the Hôtel de Paris facing the *hôtel de ville*. Due to open in Arbois any day now is a museum devoted to vines and wine.

One of the most impressive wine festivals in France is the Fête de Biou held on the first Sunday in September, when grapes built up into a massive bunch weighing about 200 lb are carried in procession through the streets of Arbois to the church and offered to St Just, patron saint of the town, after which the wine flows freely.

From Arbois, the scenic D246 leads south to the wine-growing village of Pupillin. The town produces what is acknowledged the best red wine of the Jura, and also contributes a well-known rosé. Both can be tasted at the *fruitière vinicole*. A nearby archaeological dig has revealed a number of Gallo-Roman relics. East of the village, but only approachable by road from Arbois, is the horseshoe-shaped Cirque du Fer à Cheval which forms the base of a *reculée*.

The small town of Poligny (off the N83 to the south) had its origins in the houses built by the wine growers in the shadow of the ancient fortress of Grimont, now in ruins. Washed by the river Glantine and overlooked by rocky hills, it is at the centre of a rich agricultural region – one likely explanation for its national dairy college and its title as the capital of Gruyère cheese, made in the Jura since the 13th century at *fruitières* or dairy *co-operatives*. This is the only feasible way to make it, for most dairy farmers in this part of France own only a dozen or so of the traditional red-and-white cows and it takes 600 litres of milk to make just one round Gruyère weighing about 100 lb. But there are rich vineyards in the district, too, and the red wines for which Poligny is famous can be tasted at the Caveau des Jacobins in the town.

A walk through the streets of Poligny might take in the remains of the ramparts and towers, the Chapelle de la Congregation des Vignerons, fine old houses bordering the Grande Rue, and the 15th-century Church of St

Hippolyte with its fascinating collection of statues. Equally interesting is the remarkable pharmacy, refectory, and vaulted kitchens of the 17th-century Hôtel Dieu or hospital. Poligny was the birthplace of Jacques Coitier, doctor to Louis XI, who having fallen out of favour and fearing for his life persuaded the King that he would die three days after his doctor. A short drive south-east of the town is the *reculée* called the Culée de Vaux, topped by the old priory of Vaux.

The road south to St Lothian, notable for its white wine and its 12th-century church, skirts the forest of Vaivre then continues to Passenans – where the ancient château still retains two of its round towers. Fontenay also has a château as well as a pilgrims' church and, linked to it by a tortuous byway giving panoramic views, Menetru produces a white wine much appreciated locally. Crowning a 1,500ft-high escarpment on the south-east, its steep flanks covered in vines, is Château Chalon. Still visible are the gates of the former ramparts and the ruins of the castle built to protect a Benedictine abbey founded in the 7th century and reserved for the daughters of noble families. It was the abbesses, rulers of the district round about, who planted the first vineyards. But the *vin jaune* for which Château Chalon is famous, with its curiously nutty taste, is a relatively young wine for it dates only from the 11th century. The village shares its *vin jaune appellation* with the three villages at the foot of the escarpment: Menetru, Domblans, and, with its own *fruitière vinicole*, Voiteur. To the east is the Cirque de

A cliff-top view of the Abbey of Baume les Messieurs.

Ladoye, with a grandstand view from 1,770ft up at the top and the source of one branch of the Seille at the bottom. To the west is Domblans, on the left bank of the Seille, with its 16th-century château flanked by towers where in their time Charles the Bold of Burgundy and Henri IV stayed. Near by are the wild and rocky Seille gorges. West again, at the crossroads near an 11th-century château on a wooded hill, is St-Germain-les-Arlay. Adjoining it is Arlay, noted for its wine served at the tables of the French monarchs since the 13th century, where the vineyards encircle a ruined château close by the 18th-century Château d'Arlay – set in a park and rich in period furniture.

The minor road leading south from Voiteur through Le Vernois to Pannessières skirts a steep hill ringed by vines and topped by the magnificent Château du Pin, parts of which date from 1242. Originally built by Jean de Chalon l'Antique, a man no doubt of venerable age, it was strengthened in the 15th century by the addition of the tower and huge keep.

On the Champagnole road east of Pannessières is Crançot, gateway to the impressive Cirque de Baume, from which there are immense views reaching as far as the Côte d'Or in Burgundy to the west. At the base of the cliffs is a series of high and narrow grottoes and in a striking situation the Abbey of Baume les Messieurs, with its imposing 12th-century Romanesque Abbey church decorated with statues, the tombs of the sires of Chalon, and a famous 16th-century Flemish altarpiece. The Abbey was founded in the 6th century by the Irish missionary St Columban; it was twelve monks from Baume who in 910 founded Cluny, the most influential seat of monastic learning in the medieval world. Like all other religious institutions in France, it was suppressed at the Revolution.

In the 16th century the Abbey changed its name to Baume les Messieurs

The basin of the Cirque de Baume.

when the monks were replaced by noble canons, the *messieurs*. Baume itself comes from the Latin *balma* meaning grottoes. Visitors can see the dormitory, refectory, cloister, and, in another building, a handicrafts museum. The Abbey's opposite number was Baume les Dames, north-east of Besançon.

West of Pannessières, beyond the N83, l'Etoile is dominated by the *monts* of Genezet and Musard, the second crowned by a ruined 13th-century château. With their remarkable bouquet, the white wines of l'Etoile lend themselves admirably to the infusion of sparkle, though the *appellation* – shared by the nearby communes of Quintigny and St Didier – also covers *vin de paille* and *vin jaune*.

In an open setting of vine-clad hills, Lons le Saunier is an amiable town and the chief one of the region. A spa since Roman times, it takes its suffix Saunier from the *salines* or salt springs for which it has long been famous. The thermal baths and casino are set in a splendid park on the western edge of the town, heart of which is the Place de la Liberté. In one of the arcaded houses in the Rue du Commerce off the square, Rouget de Lisle (composer of the Marseillaise) was born in 1760. The old *relais de poste* or coaching inn of the Cheval Rouge is a pleasant place to stay and a tasting of the sparkling wines for which Lons le Saunier is renowned can be had for the asking at the Maison du Vigneron in the Rue du Commerce.

The remaining leg of the route south through the vineyards – a mere 20 miles long – follows the main N83, which runs closer to the plateau than it does in the north and provides at almost every point views of a verdant landscape set against a backdrop of alpine peaks. The lower slopes of the plateau up which most of the vineyards are terraced here takes the name of Revermont or the 'back of the mountain'. Nearly all the places on or near the road produce wines covered by the Côtes du Jura *appellation*.

Beyond the ruined 12th-century castle of Beaufort is Cuiseaux, in a strange situation dominated by rocks topped by larch trees and with two surviving towers of the 36 that were once set in its ancient ramparts. There are carved choir stalls and a black Virgin in the modern church, and the Chapel of St Jacques in the cemetery – a reminder of the days when this route was thronged with pilgrims on the way to the shrine of St Jacques de Compostelle in Spain, better known to us perhaps as Santiago.

South of the stone cross of Balanod and its nearby waterfall are the southernmost vineyards in the Jura. They surround St Amour, beside the river Besançon in a restful setting at the junction of the Revermont and the plain of Bresse. This small summer resort, well known for both its marble quarries and its wine, takes its name from St Amaturas – martyred by the Roman Theban legion – whose remains were brought to the spot in the 6th century.

The vineyards of the Jura, possibly first planted by the Celts and certainly by the Gallo-Romans, repay exploration in greater detail. Apart from there being many more wines for the finding unknown outside their own localities and for meeting the modest but dedicated people who make them, there is the prospect of enjoying more of the region's beautiful scenery while savouring a wider range of its essentially genuine and delectable cuisine.

# Burgundy

If Burgundy means medieval and Renaissance masterpieces to the art lover, it evokes for the epicure richly flavoured food and classic wines. Set in an opulent landscape, the vineyards of the antique province owe their development to the great religious orders of Citeaux and Cluny, and their early success to the proximity of the medieval trade routes. Without the expertise and persevering work of the monks of these abbeys, whose first concern was holy wine for mass, Burgundy might never have produced what are probably the world's greatest wines.

The heart of the wine district is the Côte d'Or or Golden Slope, a narrow band of vineyards along the eastern flanks of the mineral-rich limestone hills rolling south from Dijon to Santenay. The northern part, called the Côte de Nuits because it is centred on Nuits-St-Georges, produces the finest red burgundies. The southern, the Côte that takes its name from the old wine capital of Beaune, makes the best white burgundies as well as some excellent reds. The Côte de Beaune, someone once said, is the Rubens to the Rembrandt of the Côte de Nuits. Its light and sensual wines have a tender fleshiness, while those of Nuits have a deeper colour and a more sombre flavour. In the old days the Beaune were called *vins de primeur* or early to mature, the Nuits *vins de garde* or slow to develop.

Neatly staked and impeccably tilled, the vineyards are constantly at risk from the vagaries of the weather. Late frosts and hail storms in spring all too often take just a few hours to destroy months of work. In a wet summer the vines may have to be sprayed perhaps a dozen times to ward off mildew, and in a cold autumn the fermenting vats frequently need to be artificially heated. The *cru* or growth of the Bordelais is replaced in Burgundy by *climat*, a word that conveys better than any other how the soil and exposure of a vineyard determine the eventual quality of the wine. Some of the vineyards are enclosed by dry stone walls, when they are called *clos*.

Partly as a result of the land of the great religious foundations being sold by the state at the Revolution and partly due to the laws governing inheritance (when a vineyard owner dies, his property must be equally divided among his heirs), no other wine district is split up among so many growers, some with plots of only two acres. Since most of them produce insufficient wine to warrant marketing it themselves, they sell it to *négociants* or middlemen.

The big difference between commune and single vineyard wines is that the first can be made from grapes grown anywhere in the parish. But the distinction is blurred by the practice adopted in the last century of communes hyphenating their names to those of their best vineyards. Even Nuits attempts to bask in the reflected glory of its prime vineyard by calling itself Nuits-St-Georges. Little-known communes also compound their own names with those of their more famous neighbours (Savigny for example has become Savigny-les-Beaune).

Even wines bearing the same vineyard *appellation* can vary considerably in quality. Over fifty growers own part of the famous vineyard of Clos

Vougeot and are entitled to put the name on their labels, no matter how small a plot they have. The middle slopes produce the best wines, but apart from this there are variations in soil, drainage, exposure to the sun, age of vines, and, equally important, in the skill and ethical standards of the growers.

Another sad fact is that to keep up with demand and save on storage many *négociants* have since 1920 been making wines to mature faster, a trend that itself accelerated after the last war. The wines may be ready to drink earlier but a built-in obsolescence leaves them with a shorter life. Not that things are as bad as they seem to have been a couple of hundred years ago. Travelling along the Côte d'Or in 1763 the cantankerous Tobias Smollett found 'the wine commonly used so weak and thin that you would not drink it in England'. Happily, some growers and *négociants* still make their wine in the old way – with a long fermentation on the skins and ample time in cask. This gives it a longer life, more colour, flavour, and body; the only disadvantage is an initial hardness from the tannin which fades with age. Even so, top vintages of the Côte d'Or have a much shorter life than fine clarets, and many classic burgundies are drunk too late – when they have died of neglect – just as many Bordeaux are drunk too early, before their prime.

Named and commune vineyards of the Côte d'Or are only planted with the three classic varieties of Pinot Noir (Noirien, Beurot, and Liebault) for red burgundy and Pinot Blanc and Chardonnay for the white. The Pinot Noir is a delicate grape that ripens early to give wines of soft style and penetrating flavour. Lesser wines of the region, many from the same varieties of grape, are covered by different *appellations*. Usually drunk young, those with the generic name *vins fins de la côte de nuits* are strong, often pleasant, and usually inexpensive. Much the same goes for Côte de Beaune and Côte de Beaune Villages. Apart from plain Bourgogne and Bourgogne Ordinaire in red, white, and rosé, there are a number of other *appellations* worth an introduction: Bourgogne Aligoté, from the Aligoté grape alone or with Pinot Chardonnay, which is now recognised as a palatable wine in its own right; the curiously named Bourgogne Passe Tout Grains, made of one third Pinot Noir and a balance of Gamay and Chardonnay; and finally red and white versions of Bourgogne Mousseux. The better commune wines need at least three years to mature and single-vineyard ones up to ten.

The small towns at the foot of the vine-clad slopes are rich in atmosphere, vinous and otherwise. Like the close-shuttered villages between them, they are peopled by easy-going individualistic folk whose appetite for food is as keen as their taste for wine. In an otherwise flowery speech given by the mayor of Nuits during a dinner in the famous Caveau Nuiton cellars, one statement of fact emerged. This was when he said it was customary for many *vignerons* of the district to clear their palates first thing in the morning with a glass of dry white burgundy. These amiable people's love of wine is only equalled by their horror of water; they even brush their teeth, so the story goes, with *un petit vin blanc de l'année*.

Nearly every restaurant in Burgundy produces the four great traditional dishes of *coq au vin* or chicken casseroled in wine; *escargots* or snails in a garlic, butter and parsley sauce; *boeuf bourguignon*, a savoury beef stew; and the *pièce de Charollais,* tender steak from the pastures to the west. But there is much more than this to the richly flavoured cuisine, famed for the variety of its wine-based sauces.

Freshwater fish comes stewed in wine, called *pauchouse* when the wine is white, *maurette* when it is red; savoury ham from the Morvan is served with parsley as *jambon persillé* or in a creamy sauce as *saupiquet;* and – this is another classic dish – salt and fresh pork, cooked together with vegetables as *potée bourguignonne.* There are egg and cheese dishes cooked in wine, hot pâtée, lamb *en croûte* or in pastry, a wide choice of *charcuterie* or pork meats, *lapin à la dijonais* or rabbit cooked in a coating of mustard, and *salade vigneron,* a green salad dressed with hot pork fat and vinegar. Two delicious cheeses are Citeaux and Soumaintrain which might be followed by a sweet such as pears cooked in wine or a *sorbet* incorporating a fruit syrup. Dijon is famous for its mustard made with white wine instead of vinegar, and for its *pain d'épice* or spiced bread made to the old recipe of wheaten flour, honey, yolks of eggs, aniseed, and allspice.

An apéritif popular with local people is *vin blanc cassis,* chilled white wine added to *crème de cassis,* a blackcurrant liqueur and often called a Kir after the late deputy-mayor of Dijon, who invented it. A similar drink is *vermouth cassis,* in which vermouth is added to the liqueur and followed by a topping of soda.

Motoring along the Côte d'Or is simple enough. The main N74 runs across the level plain at the foot of the slopes between Dijon and Beaune. West of it, and linked with it in places, is the minor road linking the wine villages and towns. South of Beaune the road pattern is more complex, some places being on the N73 La Rochepot-Nolay road and some between it and the N74 (to Chagny) to the east. The suggested drive along the Côte d'Or is one-way, north-to-south, and under 60 miles long, but it could easily be made part of a circular tour by returning north through the Arrière Côte

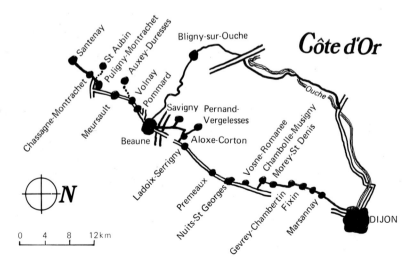

farther west. In doing this you would follow for part of the way the scenic Ouche valley, passing through the wine villages of St Romain, Meloisey, and Bouilland before joining the river at Veuvey. The yellow Michelin maps 66 and 70 cover the area. When Tobias Smollett made the bumpy six-day journey by horse-drawn cabriolet from Paris to Lyon in 1763 he chose to go by way of Dijon 'to see the wine harvest, a season of mirth and jollity among all ranks of people'. This is still the best time to come, preferably when the Fête de la Vigne is being staged in the town in early September.

Ancient capital of the Duchy of Burgundy and one of the great centres of French gastronomy, Dijon is famed for the Carolingian crypt of its St Bénigne Cathedral, its two splendid museums, and its sumptuously decorated ducal palace housing the tomb of Philip the Bold. It is now a wine-marketing rather than a wine-producing centre, though in the Middle Ages there were vineyards within as well as beyond its walls. Proof of this is the world's largest antique wine-press in the cellars of the Clos du Roi vineyard at Chenove, a southern suburb. Operated by a 20-ton weight, the press is named Margot after Marguerite, Duchess of Burgundy. The Clos du Roi and the adjoining Clos de Chapitre vineyard once provided the wines for the tables of the dukes of Burgundy and the canons of Autun.

A short way south is Marsannay-la-Côte, once renowned for its red wines but better known these days for its dry rosés – made by vinifying Pinot Noir grapes as for white wine. The famous *co-operative* in the village is happy to give visitors a taste of it. West of Marsannay is the vantage point of Mont Afrique, 2,000ft high, from which the views to the east reach as far as Mont Blanc. Rosé wines are also made at the elongated village of Couchey near by, but the Côte de Nuits proper begins at Fixin (pronounced Feessan), an *appellation* that covers red and white wines of distinction. In a pretty park is the *Reveil* or *Awakening of Napoleon*, a bronze effigy carved by the 19th-century Dijon-born sculptor François Rude. It was paid for by Noisot, captain of grenadiers in the Grande Armée, buried near by – 'standing up', as he stipulated in his will, 'facing the Emperor'.

Late last century the small town of Gevrey, at the head of the picturesque Combe de Lavaux to the south, was allowed to add to its name that of its best vineyard Chambertin. Even so, any bottle graced with the hyphenated name is unlikely to contain any Chambertin at all. Equally confusing is the practice of numerous single vineyards in the commune, all *premiers crus,* adding Chambertin to their names as well. One of the 'biggest' and most perfumed of all Côte de Nuits wines, Chambertin is said to get its name from the *champ* or field owned in medieval times by a grower named Bertin. The wine could once be aged to advantage for 50 years, but not any more.

In the upper part of the town is a 10th-century château restored in the 13th century by the monks of the great Abbey of Cluny. The interior, with its great hall and monumental staircase, is interesting enough of itself to justify a visit, quite apart from the tasting rooms in the cellars. If given the opportunity to taste Chambertin, no one should follow Napoleon's example and add water to it.

A few miles on is the Gallo-Roman village of Morey-St-Denis, where elegant white wines and heavy intensely perfumed reds are made. The famous Clos de Tart vineyard, with cellars housing a venerable wine-press, once belonged to the Bernardine nuns of the convent of Tart-le-Haut. The vigorous yet delicate wine has a rich bouquet. The nearby 38-acre vineyard of Bonnes Mares also once belonged to a religious order.

The rambling village of Chambolle-Musigny, built round its 16th-century church on the side of the hill, takes the second part of its name from the *grand cru* vineyard from which comes a roundly soft red wine with a lingering bouquet and the rare and marvellous Musigny Blanc.

The earliest systematically managed vineyards in Burgundy were those created by the monasteries a thousand years ago, the monks clearing the ground, planting the vines, and making the wine – all by painstaking trial and error. The prime example is the world-famous walled vineyard of Clos Vougeot near the village of the same name, first planted by the monks of Citeaux in the 12th century and still the largest *clos* on the Côte d'Or. Now carved up among 55 growers, the 125 acres of vines were centred on buildings housing the fermenting vats, oratory and great cellars in which, to minimise losses by pillage, the monks kept only the wine of the previous year. In 1551 the forty-eighth abbot of Citeaux, Dom Loisier, had some of the buildings pulled down to make room for the château that now dominates the vineyard. The two cellars it incorporates can hold as many as 2,000 casks of wine. Alongside the big vats in the *cuverie* are four huge wine presses, made of heart of oak and needing ten men to operate them. *Chaptalisation* is the French word for adding sugar during fermentation to increase the alcohol content of the finished wine, the maximum allowed in Burgundy is 3kg of sugar to every 100 litres of must. Surprising as it may seem, in some years even the great red wines of Vougeot lack natural vinosity and since 1790 have been chaptalised whenever necessary.

The village and *clos* take their name from the small Vouge stream that flows down from the slope, crossed in the 11th century by a toll bridge around which *auberges* and hostelries were built for travellers. On the far side of the main road, the village of Gilly-les-Citeaux surrounds the fortress built in 1305 for the abbots of Citeaux. They felt more secure there than they did at the abbey itself, isolated in the marshes some eight miles to the south-east. In 1450 the fortieth abbot, Jean Vion de Gevrey, built a cellar in the coutryard of the château where wine from Clos Vougeot was stored. Little is left of the original abbey buildings of Citeaux where the Cistercian Order was founded in 1098 and which a few centuries later had spread its influence throughout the western world.

Still to the east of the N74, the vineyards of adjoining Flagey Echezeaux are little known, perhaps because the name is considered difficult to pronounce but more likely because it is on the wrong side of the tracks – it is generally agreed that the great vineyards of the Côte d'Or are to the west of the main road.

Dom François Trouvé, last abbot of Citeaux whose authority extended to 3,000 monasteries, died in 1797 at the village of Vosne-Romanée, 'the pearl in the necklace of Burgundy', prized for its sumptuous red single vineyard wines and by those with pockets of lesser depth for its *vins de commune*.

A cluster of small vineyards covered by the separate *appellation* of Romanée-St-Vivant is centred on the fabulous *climat* of Romanée-Conti, bought in 1760 by the Prince of Conti who kept all the wine for himself, at least until it became state property at the Revolution. This was the sole quality vineyard to escape the phylloxera which devastated Burgundy in 1880. It was the ravages of old age that finally necessitated uprooting the vines in 1946.

The prosperous and ancient small town of Nuits-St-Georges owes much to the Sun King, Louis XIV, who, on recovering from a serious illness in 1686, was told by his doctor to drink its deep red and distinctly textured wine to regain his strength. From then on, everyone at court enjoyed the same diet. The 20-acre St Georges vineyard in the town's hyphenated name was first planted in the year 1,000 – no doubt by a wine-loving optimist as this was the date when many medieval people thought the world would end.

As well as still red wines, abundant in tannin and therefore needing five to ten years to develop, Nuits makes a sparkling red burgundy said to make even the strongest women weak. All of them can be sampled at the tasting cellars in the *hôtel de ville* or town hall.

Surrounding the pretty Church of St Symphorien are the premises of the *négociants* and on the outskirts are the ruins of the Roman city of Les Bolards, with a little museum housing the relics found there. The Haut Côte de Nuits in the hills around Villers-la-Faye, reached on the D8 from Nuits, is as noted for its scenery as for its wines. From 1250, the vineyards of Premeaux (on the main road south of Nuits) were renowned, and the best wines – such as those from the Clos de la Maréchale – are still thought outstanding. The swimming pool in the small village is fed by a warm-water spring.

The Côte de Nuits ends at Comblanchien, known for its passably good *ordinaires* and for its giant quarries from which came the decorative stone used on the façade of the Opéra in Paris.

The northernmost vineyards of the Côte de Beaune are those around the hamlet of Ladoix on the main road and the large village of Serrigny to the west of it, twinned as Ladoix-Serrigny. The two make some pleasantly perfumed red wines and excellent whites with a curious nutty flavour. They can be sampled at the cellars of St Bacchus, Edmond Cornu, or André Nudant.

West of the main road at the foot of what is locally called 'the mountain' is Aloxe-Corton (pronounced Alosse), another hyphenated name celebrated for the trinity of *grands crus* vineyards: Corton, Charlemagne, and the hybrid Corton-Charlemagne – the last two produce great golden wines high in alcohol and full of aromatic savour. The vineyard said to have been owned by Charlemagne – he is reputed to have forbidden the trampling of grapes because he believed it detrimental to the wine – is now split up between various *négociants*. Good wines taste best when shared and it is typical of Voltaire that he should serve Beaujolais to his friends while himself drinking Corton. Standing back from the N74 at the opening of the pretty

33

valley of Fontaine-Froide, Pernand-Vergelessès is an attractive village of Celtic origin which produces noble red wines that leave an aftertaste of raspberries.

Centred on its pretty 14th-century château, Savigny-les-Beaune to the west of the main road is the only place on the Côte d'Or where white Bourgogne Mousseux is made from the vineyards that extend west along the Rhoin valley. This and some excellent still red and white wines can be tasted at the Petitjean cellars. The Count de la Loyere, owner of the château in the 19th century, is said to have been the first grower to plant vines in rows. What is certain is that it was he who invented the vine plough. Ringed by vines and still circular in plan, the old and proud city of Beaune typifies all the charm of provincial France. In the Logis du Roi, the former palace of the all-powerful dukes of Burgundy, is a fascinating wine museum; there are fine tapestries and frescoes in the 12th-century Romanesque Church of Notre Dame; and from the ramparts are commanding views of the steep roofs of quaint old houses lining concentric streets.

Like other towns and large villages along the Côte d'Or, subterranean Beaune is honeycombed with cellars in which sleeps a veritable river of wine. The first cellars were dug to house the *grands crus* of the dukes but many others, some two storeys deep, were hollowed out by monks to take the wines of their abbeys and are as beautifully vaulted and colonnaded as crypts. They demonstrate an almost mystical reverence for wine.

'Proud Marguerite' included Flanders as part of her dowry to 'Philip the Bold' of Burgundy. So, when the Duke's Chancellor Nicolas Rolin decided to build a home for the poor and the infirm in Beaune, it was logical that the building should be modelled on the hospital of St Jacques at Valenciennes, now in France but then in Flanders, and that he should employ a Flemish architect to carry out the work. The hospice was completed in the winter of 1442, the chapel consecrated on 31 December that year, and the first of the infirm along with the first six Sisters of Charity from Malines installed on New Year's day, 1443. Since then, with little change, the nuns have continued their charitable work, every New Year's eve finding on their beds three francs as symbolic payment. Based on that worn in the *béguinages* of Flanders, their dress has also remained unchanged: white coif and woollen gowns – blue for winter, white for summer.

Among the priceless works of art in the hospice is the painting of the *Last Judgement* by Roger van der Weyden and the historic *Book of Gold*. Over the years many vineyards along the Côte d'Or have been given or bequeathed to the hospice – more correctly, the Hôtel Dieu. The wines from them, still known by the names of the donors, are auctioned off annually, usually on the third Sunday in November and always *à la chandelle* – the successful buyer being the one who bids last before the candle goes out. Prices are of course high since they reflect motives of prestige and charity, and form the hospice's only source of income. For a few francs anyone may go into the cellars and taste the wines offered for auction.

Beaune stages its wine fair in mid June – though savoury regional dishes can be sampled at any time in its historic restaurants, and many of the wines in the cellars of Batistines, the 12th-century Cave du Bourgogne, the Cave des Cordeliers in an ancient convent, and many other places. Some of them will house the soft and delicately perfumed wines of the many single vine-yards that still exist in the commune.

On the N73 south-west of Beaune is Pommard, backed by two hills of ochre-coloured soil and christened Pomone, god of fruits and gardens, by the ancient Romans. Its 24 named vineyards produce a strong wine which needs several years in bottle to mellow its initial hardness. In season, the local *comité d'accueil* operates a stand for tastings.

A mile or two south is delightful Volnay, built on a hill around its 13th-century church and producing elegant red wines. The best vineyard, high up the slope below the statue of Notre Dame des Vignes, is les Caillerets, but the Clos de Chênes is a close runner-up. Records of 1395 mention the reigning Pope, King of France, and noblemen as buyers of Volnay. Louis XI, having gained control of Burgundy on the death of Philip the Bold, commanded perhaps by way of celebration that the whole of the 1477 vintage be sent to his château on the Loire. Growers in the village who welcome callers at their cellars include Louis Glantenay, Emile Bouley, Henri Boillot, and Michel Pont.

Before the Revolution, Volnay was noted more for its white wines, and the small town of Meursault, to the south, for its reds. The fashion then was for pink wines the colour of a partridge's eye (*oeil de perdrix*), a term now used for some sparkling burgundies.

The church spire of charming Meursault, a landmark for miles around, overshadows the keep of the old castle housing the municipal offices. Adjoining the castle are extensive cellars dug by Cistercian monks in the 14th century which contain a varied collection of antique wine bottles. This is one place where the dry, steely white wine can be tasted, another being the Maison du Meursault in the town. The distinguished wines have a hint of peaches in the flavour and a powerful bouquet. They are deservedly famous but hardly anyone outside the district seems to have heard of the top-quality red wine from the Santenots vineyard. Meursault has the distinction of being the only place in Burgundy to produce *tête de cuvée* red wines as well as white.

Also little known are the red wines of nearby Monthelie, mentioned as long ago as the 9th century; between Easter and All Saints they can be sampled at the *caves* in the village.

Auxey-Duresses, dominated on the south by the bulk of Montmellian, occupies the site of a Roman encampment at the opening of the valley leading to the feudal castle of La Rochepot, rebuilt in the 15th century and one of the most interesting in Burgundy. The village of Auxey has no *grands crus* but the flowery wines are highly thought of in France and have their own *appellation*. They can be tried at the *caveau communal*.

The vineyards around the hamlet of Blagny, on the eastern slopes of Montmellian, produce red and white wines – the exquisite but little-discovered Blagny Blancs being said not only to rival those of Meursault in flavour but to outlive them, too. Having a better exposure – all the finest wines come from the slopes – but a little-known name, they are likely to be better value for money. The adjoining hamlet of Gamay gave its name to the generous grape, banned in Burgundy by Philip the Bold in 1395, on which the fame of Beaujolais is founded. From the extensive walled vineyards around the twin villages of Puligny-Montrachet on either side of the road linking Chagny and Nolay comes the magnificent white wine of Montrachet, (pronounced 'Mon-Raché), acknowledged the greatest dry-white table-wine in the world, deeply rounded, with a subtle melody of flavours, and a lovely smell. It comes into its own after about eight or nine years in bottle.

The greatest name is of course the 19-acre Montrachet vineyard, its vines exposed to the golden rays from sunrise to sunset. Next best are the three plots with names hyphenated to it: Bâtard, Chevalier, and Bienvenues-Bâtard. The red wines of Chassagne can be pleasant though they are rarely heard of. In the attractive village of Puligny, the houses of the wine growers are easy to recognise: since the subsoil is too porous for cellars, the wines have to be stored above ground and the only recourse for the *vignerons* is to live on the first floor – reached by an external staircase.

Covered by the Côte de Beaune *appellation,* the wines of St Aubin between Puligny-Montrachet and La Rochepot are much less expensive than their famous neighbours, yet reflect them in their flavour and bouquet. They can be sampled at the Lamy or Roux cellars in the village.

At the southern limit of the Côte de Beaune is picturesque Santenay. It is a small wine town and spa, on the left bank of the Dheune, complete with 14th-century castle, thermal baths, and casino. From its vineyards, sheltered by a half-circle of hills, come fruity and light red and crisply dry white wines. The Côte d'Or is little over 30 miles from north to south, yet as Cyrus Redding wrote in 1833, 'there is an infinite variety in the nature of the soil, the aspect, the season, the plant and mode of culture, as well as the making, each and all affecting the quality of the wines more than others on account of their great delicacy.' This makes these vineyards much less predictable than those elsewhere but consequently more exciting to explore.

# Beaujolais

Thirst-quenching beaujolais is obviously one of the best-known wines, yet it comes from one of the least-known vineyard areas of France. Ignored by most guide books and bypassed by the traffic rushing along the Saône valley, the sharply contoured hills that tumble down from the forested Monts du Beaujolais towards the river form a compact and admirably modelled region of mellow charm – decorated with the red roofs and old stones of unpretentious villages and small towns, and laced by winding roads which in places can be astonishingly steep. Just as surprising are the contrasting views: narrow and enclosed at one point, spacious and far-reaching at another.

Nearly every village has a tasting cellar but places to stay are more limited; those that do exist are homely, even rustic, but the scenery is delightful and the people, most of whom live by wine, are engagingly frank and friendly. To explore such a little-visited part of France while educating one's palate to the subtle differences of *crus* with well-worn names is an oddly rewarding experience.

In this geologically jumbled landscape, well ordered rows of vines cover the steep granite slopes as far as the eye can see. What is lacking is trees, bearing out the local adage that the only shade acceptable to the vines is that cast by the *vignerons*. Even the speedy growth in the acreage of newly planted vines does not compare with the sensational rise in popularity of the wine that is eventually pressed from them.

At one time beaujolais was the standard carafe wine in the restaurants of nearby Lyon, when it was usually served in *pots* of 46cl – a bottle size that is enjoying a revival. Some time later the wine reached Paris, the rest of France, and finally other countries. In post-war England its success was phenomenal. The grape harvest in the Beaujolais is early and is sometimes over by mid September. Because it is vinified quickly, the *nouveau* on sale from mid November needs to be drunk before the year is out. Its short life is due to its accelerated *cuvage* of four to five days, which produces its characteristic light colour and makes it quick to mature. All this concerns only common-or-garden beaujolais and a few beaujolais villages: happily the better growths are vatted for much longer, which partly explains why they are so much 'bigger' than their second cousins. Genuine beaujolais is made wholly from the generous Gamay – the vine Philip the Bold of Burgundy banned throughout his domain in 1395 – though much of what is sold is stretched with wines from the Languedoc or North Africa, and some contains no beaujolais at all. Writing in 1940, Maurice Healy confirmed the fact that, in England at any rate, its provenance seems to have been doubtful from the start.

Does the wine really belong in its official category of a Burgundy? The old cliché that beaujolais is one of three rivers flowing into Lyon (the others being the Saône and the Rhône) does at least suggest that by geography and tradition the region comes within the orbit of the city, a mere stone's throw south. Its vines grow on granite, too, not limestone like those further north, and its grape is the Gamay Noir *à jus blanc*, not the Pinot Noir of Burgundy.

The answer must be that beaujolais – uncomplicated, refreshingly acid, and richly coloured – is a wine that can stand by itself.

At the top of the quality scale are nine named commune *appellations,* the wines entitled to them usually containing not less than 10° of alcohol. Within each of these delimited areas there are, of course, named vineyards. Next in order of superiority are beaujolais villages, followed by beaujolais supérieur and, finally, plain made-for-quaffing beaujolais, one third of which is produced by *co-operatives.* All this refers to the red, though a small amount of white and rosé is made in the northern part of the region.

A solid stomach makes for a solid conscience say the open-faced folk of Beaujolais. Perhaps because of their warm climate they may not have the capacity of the trenchers in other parts of France but they certainly eat well. Differing little from the rest of the Lyonnais, their cuisine is essentially simple and genuine. As one would expect, many dishes incorporate wine: even the popular *andouillette,* a coarsely cut and tasty chitterling sausage, is often cooked in beaujolais. *Ecrevisses,* or crayfish, from the many streams are often served with cream or cooked with trout in a *coussinet* or pastry case. The beef of the nearby Charollais district, succulent and tender, appears on the menu in numerous forms. There is game from the forested mountains in season, savoury trout from the Azergues river flowing down from the Monts du Beaujolais, and a wide range of cheeses (including tiny rounds made of goats' milk). Many of the vegetables are early *primeurs* ripened by the near-Mediterranean sun. Beaujolais is one of the few red wines light enough to drink with the plump free-range chickens of the region – which are often served, as in other parts of the Lyonnais, as *poularde demi-deule* or *en chemise,* with slivers of truffle inserted between the skin and the flesh.

*Ordinaire* or commune red beaujolais is often brought to the restaurant tables chilled in summer, perfect on a hot day. The best vineyards are in the Haut Beaujolais north of Villefranche-sur-Saône, an area no more than 20 miles long by 10 miles wide, its accepted northern boundary being the Arlois stream, its southern the Nizerand, both flowing east to the Saône. South of Villefranche is the Bas Beaujolais, pleasant touring country but one producing unremarkable wines with a *gout de terroir* or earthy taste added by the chalky soil. In the northern half, the vines climb on the west up to a height of 1,500ft. Those of the lesser growths are pruned by the Guyot system and trained along wires, those of the top quality vineyards by the Gobelet, in which the freestanding vines are usually no taller than the *vigneron's* knee.

Motoring in the Beaujolais is not difficult but the semi-alpine roads tend to make it slow. Gateway to the region from the north is Crêches, on the N6 south of Macon. From Crêches the D31 winds west in company with the Arlois stream to Chanes, starting point of the road which – though sections are numbered differently – meanders south through the vineyards of the nine commune *appellations* of the Haut Beaujolais before rejoining the N6 at Villefranche. The yellow Michelin map 73 covers the whole area, though the road pattern is so contorted that one drawn to twice the scale would be at least twice as helpful.

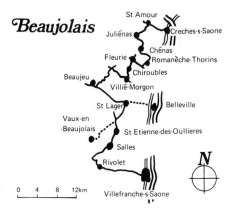

**Beaujolais**

St Amour
Juliénas
Creches-s-Saone
Chénas
Fleurie
Romanèche-Thorins
Beaujeu
Chiroubles
Villié-Morgon
St Lager
Belleville
Vaux-en
-Beaujolais
St Etienne-des-Oullieres
Salles
Rivolet
Villefranche-s-Saone

0   4   8   12km

N

South of Chanes is St Amour, the northernmost top growth which produces the popular red – one of the lightest of the nine – and also a notable white wine from the Chardonnay grape. Both can be tasted at the *caveau* in the village. Most of the vineyards, on pebbly granitic and slatey soil, cover the eastern and south-eastern slopes of the 750ft-high hill on the south.

Ten minutes' up-and-down motoring leads to Juliénas, another big name. The long-lasting yet volatile wine is claimed by some to be the best in the region. In the village is the picturesque Maison de la Dime dating from 1647, and, decorated in shockingly bad taste, the tasting cellar in the Vieille Eglise. The local *co-operative* has a cellar open to visitors, too, in the Château du Bois de la Salle.

The next *appellation* commune on the way south is Chénas (pronounced Cheynah), with its Caveau du Cru Chénas. Outstanding named growths are the *domaines* of Journets and Berthets. Nearby Moulin à Vent, its vineyards established as long ago as the 12th century, its vines a finer version of Gamay called Petit Gamay, is a name that everyone knows. The deep-coloured and rounded wine needs four or five years to mature. This being the top Beaujolais *appellation,* there are sound commercial reasons why the wines from the best part of the Chénas vineyards are sold under the name of its more famous neighbour. Near the tasting cellar at the foot of the *vieux moulin,* a disappointingly dull structure, is the house where Benoit Raclet carried out his viticultural experiments and, say local growers, 'saved our vines'. The most important vineyards are Clos Rochette, Château des Jacques, Clos du Grand Carquelin, and Grand Clos de Rochegrès.

Over to the east is Romanèche-Thorins, where most of the wines are also marketed as Moulin à Vent, with its museum devoted to journeymen *(compagnonnage),* and, beside the N6, the tasting cellars of the Union des Viticulteurs du Moulin à Vent. Thorin wines, their flavour very much influenced by the manganese in the sub-soil hereabouts, have been popular for centuries, partly because they are among the most drinkable of the region, and partly because in former times they were the ones most often served to travellers (journeymen included) at the *auberges* on the ancient trade route along the adjoining Saône valley that is now replaced by the N6.

West of Thorins, at the centre of the big delimited area that takes its name, is Fleurie, probably the *appellation* most liked in Britain and certainly the king of the truly characteristic beaujolais: fruity, full bodied, yet smooth. The manganese ore, mined in the locality throughout the 19th century, undoubtedly gives breeding to the wine. One of the best vineyards is Clos de la Roilette, but the biggest producer is the famous *co-operative* (which welcomes all comers to its cellars).

Built round the curious spire of its church, Chiroubles has two cellars – the Terrasse and that of the local *co-operative* – offering a tasting of the soft and distinctive wine, usually the lowest priced of the finer growths. It needs to be drunk young, preferably as it used to be – on tap from the barrel. In the village square is a statue of Pulliat, the first grower in the Beaujolais to plant vines grafted on American root stocks after the phylloxera disaster in the late 19th century.

Among the wines waiting to be sampled at the Caveau de Morgon at Villié-Morgon a few miles south-east is likely to be one locally known as *vin de Py*. It comes from the slopes separating Villié from Morgon proper, where the most extensive quality vineyard is that surrounding the Château de Pizay. Not far away is the fine *vignoble* of Château Bellevue, owned by the Princess of Lieven. Few people will need reminding that Morgon is one of the top growths; the wine has a lovely colour, is full bodied – even hard when young – and being left in cask for up to nine months before being bottled is one of the few beaujolais that improves with keeping. By contrast, Villié-Morgon, a typical example of the Burgundian practice of a lesser name linking itself with a better-known one, is usually lighter.

A drive west over the easy Col des Truges and along a narrow valley brings one to the historic small town of Braujeu, which gave its name to both the region and one of the most ancient baronies of France. At the edge of the town-hall square, centred on a statue of Gnafron, the celebrated puppet of Lyon, are the tasting cellars of the Temple de Bacchus, though the wine grown hereabouts is unremarkable. As well as the ruins of an ancient castle put out of commission by Richelieu in 1611, a church dating from 1134, and a folklore museum, Beaujeu has a couple of excellent restaurants. In the town is a hospice which holds an annual sale of wines from its donated vineyards, the proceeds as at Beaune being used to care for the poor and the needy.

One of the few roads here which can justifiably be called 'main' is that cutting east-west across the region from Beaujeu to Belleville. Founded as a free town by Humbert, one of the all-powerful 12th-century sires, Beaujeu is now sandwiched between the busy N6 and the Autoroute du Sud. Beside the N6 (north of the town) is the Maison du Beaujolais, where it is said to be possible – though for motorists not advisable – to taste every wine of the district. At a midway point just off the road is St Lager, a village from which there are wide views of the surrounding landscape. To the south-east is the strange rock formation known as Mont Brouilly topped by the pilgrimage chapel built by the growers of a century ago to exorcise the *oidium* then attacking the vines, and dedicated to Notre Dame du Raisin or Our Lady of the Grape. Here, in early September the *vignerons* give thanks in anticipation of a good harvest and also no doubt for the mad scramble for the heady beaujolais nouveau that usually follows one.

From the vines on the lower slopes comes Côte de Brouilly, a wine with more character and a separate *appellation* from just plain Brouilly, though this too is one of the top growths even if it is the southernmost. Both can be tasted in the Cuvage de Brouilly cellars at St Lager. The wines from the named vineyard of Château de Briante near Brouilly can be outstanding, but a sight not to be missed are the huge cellars of the Château de la Chaize, yet another famous name. South, beyond Odenas and St Etienne, is the hamlet of La Talharde from which the D49, an easier road than most, follows the Vauxonne valley west to Vaux en Beaujolais, said to have been the place satirised in Gabriel Chevalier's famous novel. Most of the humour in the book derives from the clash between those for and those against the erection in the village of a *vespasienne* or *pissoir*, pompously described by the *Times* of the day as a 'small public edifice'. The title is commemorated by the Cave de Clochemerle cellars in Vaux.

A byway route below St Etienne passes through Salles, built round a 12th-century church in a wide valley, then continues through a scenic countryside – inset with the splendid feudal castle of Montmélas, enclosed by a double line of ramparts – to Rivolet. From there it is a straightforward drive to Villefranche, the chief town of the Beaujolais and a market for the wines – its streets impregnated with their vinous bouquet. In the Grande Rue are some quaint old houses with enclosed courtyards and the 11th-century Church of Notre Dame des Marais. The Church gets its name from marshes long since drained that were created by the Morgon stream crossing the town to flow into the Saône near the municipal bathing beach. Two note-worthy features of the Church are the flamboyant west front and the elaborate vaulting of the nave.

# Rhône valley

Cleaving its way between the Massif Central and the foothills of the Alps, the majestic Rhône flows south from Lyon through a varied and contrasting landscape: from gently pastoral to wildly dramatic. Narrow rocky terraces ablaze in spring with peach and apricot blossom give way in the lower reaches to the luminous and fragrant hills of Provence, baked by the sun and echoing to the harsh chant of cicadas.

A great natural artery of France, the Rhône is steeped in history. From the earliest times, the valley has been important as a trade route linking the North Sea with the Mediterranean and as a thoroughfare from which the Roman legions and Christian missionaries fanned out into Gaul. Not surprisingly, it was also one of the main centres for worship of the Persian sun-god Mithras. Nowadays, the river is used to provide hydro-electric power on a vast scale and is dammed in so many places as to constitute a gigantic staircase of water. But as well as being an economic artery the valley is an elongated vineyard, some parts of it established over 2,000 years ago. No other waterway possesses such a range of great wines, from pale gold through to garnet red, some made in such small quantities that the only feasible place to taste them is where they are made. The vines grow in an astonishing variety of situations, micro-climates, and soils, yet each wine has an easily recognisable purity of savour. Less extensive than they were before the phylloxera decimated them in 1880, they still stretch for 125 miles along the river between Vienne and Avignon, passing through no less than 138 communes.

A few of the wines are simple *vins de pays* but many are covered by the generic *appellation* Côtes du Rhône (near meaningless, considering the range of areas it covers). Sometimes there is the addition on the label of one of the *départements* through which the river passes or the name of the locality. The former downgrades the *appellation,* the latter upgrades it. Finally, there are nine wines entitled to an *appellation* of their own as well as the generic name. The quality districts are clustered in the north between Vienne and Valence, mostly occupying steep terraces. They produce the finest, firmest, and most stylish wines, mostly from white Viognier and the unique red Syrah vines. The middle section of the valley opens out and in many places is better suited to other crops. In the south, on rolling hills of stony alluvial soil washed down by the Rhône, are the big production areas from which come soft full wines like Châteauneuf. These are made from a multiplicity of grape varieties, two of the most frequently used being the rich soft Grenache and Bourboulenc.

Rhône wines tend to be higher in alcohol and fuller but less subtle in flavour than those from other areas. Kept in bottle over a long period, the best achieve a complexity and harmony to justify the high reputation they once held in wine mythology.

Long, hot, and dry summers and mild winters are the main climatic characteristics. The vines cling to tripod stakes in the northern part of the valley, punctuated in its lower reaches by rows of cypress and poplar trees close-planted as windbreaks to protect the early vegetables and fruit from the mistral wind that comes howling down the valley in spring and autumn. In this area, the vines have evolved a tough tannin in the skins of their grapes which shields the pulp and gives force to the wine. The mistral, which Arthur Young writing in 1789 called the *vent de bize*, takes its name from the Latin *magistral* or master wind. It blew for several days when he was at Orange, clearing the sky and tempering the heat but more penetratingly drying than he had any conception of, 'seeming to desiccate all interior humidity'. In the southern part of the valley, particularly, the vines – grown as low bushes without support of any kind – have a long life and remain fruitful for 80 years, compared with only 25 farther north.

Two main highways flank the Rhône. The Gallic chariot-road the Romans rebuilt on the left bank to link their adopted port of Marseille with Lyon, capital of Gaul, is now the fast N7. But the *route nationale* passing closest to the vineyards is the N86', the Rhône 'corniche' on the right bank, not only more picturesque but quieter, by day or night. The Michelin map 93 covers the vineyards from Vienne, where the suggested drive starts, down to the district around Avignon, where it ends. Catering for travellers is a long established tradition on this fascinating thoroughfare, which passes through no less than seven *départements*: Rhône, Loire, Isère, Ardèche, Drôme, Vaucluse, and Gard. Each has a savoury dish or two to add to each course on the bill of fare. The valley is a true horn of plenty, the food – as astonishingly varied as the wines – changing along with the vegetation as one goes south.

Many meals begin with *ris de veau* or sweetbreads *en terrine* flavoured with sorrel or *en brioche* with *morilles*, a type of mushroom; artichokes stuffed with herb-flavoured pork; *pistou* soup; *chardons à la moelle* or edible thistles cooked in bone marrow; soufflé of chicken livers; omelette with truffles; thrush pâté flavoured with gin; *friture du Rhône*, a fish fry; or savoury sliced sausage such as *cochonailles* or *cervelas*. Chicken forms the basis of many dishes, sometimes served with crayfish as *poulet aux écrevisses*. Trout from the streams of the Ardèche are stuffed and braised, and the excellent beef and lamb are cooked in numerous ways but most often roasted with herbs. In the autumn there is a vast amount of game, though here the term is stretched to include species we leave strictly alone. *Lapereau* or young rabbit is often cooked *en compote* or with lemon as *au citron; perdrix* or partridge with cabbage, and chicken or unspecified species of small game birds are served as *coquelet aux oignons*. *Grive aux raisins* or thrush with grapes and *alouettes sur gratin dauphinois* (larks on a bed of sliced potatoes baked in milk) serve to remind one that here, although French children are taught to protect wild birds, a man will eat a dozen warblers at a sitting.

The Rhône valley is noted for its *primeurs*, early vegetables and fruit that ripen much earlier than elsewhere. As well as asparagus, artichokes, and salad vegetables available almost year-round, they include luscious melons, table grapes, cherries, apricots, peaches, pears, and prunes. There are many cheeses, too, though most common are *banons* and *poivre d'âne*, both made from goats' milk. The Ardèche, along the right bank of the Rhône, grows most of the edible chestnuts in France. Called *marrons*, these are used as stuffing, and for dessert when creamed or *glacé*.

On the left bank of the Rhône, animated Vienne has preserved many relics of its historic past: a great Roman theatre, a temple dedicated to Augustus, and a Gothic cathedral and cloister. It is a noted centre of gastronomy, too, one temple to which is the great restaurant run by Madame Point, who continues the tradition established by her late husband and *maître-cuisinier* Fernand. The restaurant takes its name from the pyramid said to mark the grave of Pontius Pilate, one-time Roman governor of the city. Vienne was known for centuries as 'la Vineuse', the Romans then complaining that its wines had a natural taste of pitch.

But the northernmost Côtes du Rhône vineyards now begin on the western side of the river three miles downstream from Vienne at Ampuis, founded in 600BC by Phoenician contemporaries of those who settled in Marseille. Backed by a group of low hills, the last granitic out-thrusts of the Massif Central, the village, with its ruined fortifications and 15th-century houses, is famous for its 'roasted slope' of Côte Rôtie – facing south-south-east and therefore in full sun for most of the day – from which come full-bodied red wines with a unique bouquet and from 12° to 14° of alcohol. The

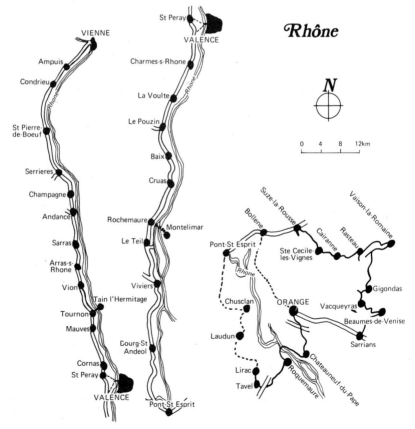

two best parts of these steeply terraced and difficult-to-cultivate vineyards, among the most ancient in France, are called Brune and Blonde – names that refer not to local girls but to the local soil. The brunette has a higher iron content (and conversely less lime) and so makes a better wine, though most Côte Rôtie is a blend of the two. Made in the traditional way, a good Côte Rôtie has a life as long as any Burgundy. At nine or ten years old it can be superb. In days gone by it spent five or more years in cask before being bottled. This same wine (known no doubt by a different name) was drunk and enjoyed by both Pliny and Plutarch. The vineyards, probably planted by the Celts in pre-Roman days, were of great renown in AD100. One place to taste the wines is at the premises of Vidal Fleury in Ampuis. On the same side of the river a few miles south is the old port of Condrieu. This is an agreeable little town built around a ruined castle and known for its dry white wine from the golden Viognier grape. Since the wine is not normally a good traveller most of it is drunk locally. It can be sampled at the Château du Rozay. Condrieu is the home of many of the skilled pilots operating on the Rhône. Among them, a medieval custom that still survives is to refer to the left bank of the river as *empire* and to the right bank as *royaume* or kingdom.

Terraced up a south-facing granite hill downstream between Verin and St Michel is the small pre-phylloxera Viognier vineyard of Château Grillet, producing one of the great white wines of France. Because so little of it is made it is one of the rarest – and most talked about – of wines. Velvety and full bodied, with up to 15° of alcohol, it has the mayflower smell typical of the Viognier and a tangy bitter-sweet finish. South again is St Pierre de Boeuf, centred on a 15th-century chapel at the opening of the beautiful gorge of Malleval, and the picturesque small town of Serrières. This was another haunt of river sailors and there is a museum recalling their life and ancient customs, a church housing the mummified bodies of the dead, and, more cheerful, shady quays beside the Rhône.

Beyond the riverside Louis XIII Château of Peyraud and the pretty Church of Champagne is delightfully named Andance, its ancient castle ruins above the vineyards looking across the river to the hilltop keep of the 11th-century lords of Albon – who by their territorial greed created the province of Dauphiny. The vineyard areas west of the N86 increase in size once the highway has crossed the Cance flowing down from Annonay to join the Rhône. Facing St Vallier on the opposite bank, the Côtes du Rhône slopes, backing Sarras and Ozon, thin out around Arras only to grow more extensive again south of Vion (at which point the velvety and full-bodied wines – the reds almost a mauve – take on the *appellation locale* of St Joseph). On this stretch the valley gradually narrows, its flanks closing in abruptly at Tournon, a cheerful town of medium size in an impressive situation dominated by its Renaissance château. One of the figures portrayed in the castle is Hélène, whose history – related by the regal Marguerite of Navarre in her *Mémoires* – may have provided the story line for Shakespeare's Ophelia. The mariner's cross in the town museum is typical of those that once decorated the prows of river boats hereabouts, its crossbar hung with such familiar tools as drill, hammer, and pincers, and its upright topped by a weather cock. At weekends from July to September, a rewarding day excursion from Tournon (a pleasant place to stay) is the ride on the *petit train à vapeur* west along the beautiful Doux Valley.

The slopes cloaked in Syrah vines below Tournon on this side of the river also produce St Joseph, the white wine that goes down particularly well with the trout from the mountain streams of the Ardèche. White or red, this is an *appellation* rarely if ever seen in Britain now, though from the 18th century to Victorian times it was imported in quantity (under the name of the nearby village of Mauves).

In 1224 the knight Henri Gaspard de Sterimberg, sickened by the horrors of the Albigensian Crusade in which he had taken part, fulfilled his vow to found a hermitage on the summit of the hill, planted with vines since pre-Roman times. Red Hermitage from Syrah, 'the manliest of wines' according to Saintsbury, and the dry white from Viognier have a unique flavour and bouquet and an alcohol content as high as 15°. Few are left to age as they used to be, when 40-year-old Hermitage would throw a crust to rival any vintage port. The red was so well liked in 19th-century England that even the great clarets were liberally stretched with it before being shipped to London.

Tain, bisected by the busy N7, has good restaurants but is no place to spend the night. Even so, no one should leave before tasting the wines (the *caveaux* or cellars of Le Pressoir, Jaboulet Aîné, and Chapoutier welcome visitors) or seeing the *taurabole*, a Mithraic altar dating from AD184. The Persian cult of Mithras, contemporary with and a serious rival to Christianity, was handed on from ancient Greece to Rome and from there to Gaul by the

The cultivated hillsides skirting Tain.

colonizing Romans. Except for the bas relief found in the Capitol in Rome and now in the Louvre, the underground sanctuary at Capua near Naples, and the *tauraboles* at Tain and in Armagnac, few traces remain of this great 'religion of the sun' (with its ceremony at which a bull was slain and the converts sprinkled with its blood). The Crozes-Hermitage vineyards, set in some of the Rhône valley's most attractive scenery, enclose those of Tain on the north, east, and south, and cover a much larger area. The Syrah, Marsanne, and Roussane vines being planted on clay and sand produce lighter yet still distinctive wines.

Beyond the castle restaurant of Châteaubourg on the right bank of the Rhône below Tournon, but away from the river, is the small village of Cornas, backed by the last foothills of the Cevennes and famed for its virile and austere red wine grown for the most part on what was once a river bed. This is another *appellation* in its own right. The name of the village, appropriately enough, is Celtic for 'scorched earth'.

Crowning a 650ft-high rock pinnacle rising up from the valley to the south is the ruined 12th-century Château of Crussol. From the keep (it takes an hour to climb up to it) there are views of Valence terraced along the opposite bank of the Rhône and in the distance the white peaks of the Alps. At the foot of the rock is St Peray, in the charming Mialan valley. Its vineyards, planted with Roussane and Marsanne varieties, were first mentioned in the records of the Abbey of St Chaffre at Monastier on 1 August 958, and the golden wines from them were later praised in the Ingoldsby Legends. These come *nature* or still, and also in a sparkling version that has been made since 1929 by the *méthode champenoise*. During the French Revolution, every commune named after a religious or royal personage was rechristened: St Peray becoming Peray Vin Blanc. Not a lot of the wine is made, so it is worth stopping to taste it at the Verilhac cellars.

Below the ancient village of Charmes is La Voulte, an historic settlement in an attractive situation above the Rhône, its houses spilling down the rock crowned by its old quarter and a 16th-century ducal chapel, its vineyards producing a modest *vin du pays*. Near a vast dam spanning the river downstream, Baix is a pleasant riverside town with some old houses and a ruined 16th-century château. After the huge limestone quarries of Cruas comes Rochemaure, at one end of another huge dam. The Rhône flows more swiftly here, its waters swollen by the streams tumbling down from the Ardèche.

Facing Montelimar, to which it is linked by a bridge, Rochemaure is in a curious situation and one of the most beautiful in the valley. Topped by feudal ruins, it consists of one long narrow street closed at each end by a fortified gate. On the hill, the ruined castle is separated from its keep by an astonishing volcanic cleft with near-vertical walls called the Chaine des Coirons which extends from the riverside west to Mont Mezenc.

Dominated by the Cathedral of St Vincent, the attractive little town of Viviers on a rocky plateau at the junction of two arms of the Rhône was once the capital of the old province of Vivarais (Ardèche), to which it gave its name. From the parvis of the Cathedral, or from the terrace of the nearby *château vieux* above the steep streets, there are fine views of the red roofs of the lower town and of the valley beyond. Linking the two is the picturesque Grande Rue, bordered by classical mansions. Christianity sounded the death knell of paganism at the ancient Gallo-Roman town of Bourg-St-Andeol, ten miles or so to the south, which takes the name of the man martyred there in 208. Reminders of the antique cults it supplanted are the bas relief of Mithras on one of the fountains, and the marble statue of Diane the huntress decorating a square near by. The beautiful churches in the town, one named after Polycarpe, Bishop of Smyrna, and another after Andeol, the first evangelist he sent to convert the Gauls, commemorate the victory. On the west is the plateau des Grads, rich in Neolithic relics and subterranean grottoes, the most impressive of which is the Aven de Morzal.

The N86 leaves the river to rejoin it farther south at Pont St Esprit, an important road junction and an old fortified town which gets its name from the remarkably long bridge spanning one of the swifter reaches of the Rhône. It was built in 1265 by bridge-building friars and dedicated to the Holy Ghost. This and the N94 link it to Bollene, over to the east on the canal du Rhône. At the end of a byway off D17 to the north of Bollene is the oldest village in France, the troglodyte settlement of Barry. Its dwellings, hewn out of the rock, have been inhabited since Neolithic times. From Bollene south to Orange is a straightforward if not particularly interesting drive, on the N7, of about 20 miles. You would be better advised to make a semi-circular tour which, although it adds another 40 miles to the journey, leads you to the scenic countryside to the east – before rejoining the N7 at Orange. The route links up some charming hill villages in a little-known part of France which lies at the heart of the Côtes du Rhône wine production.

Reached by a road along the south bank of the river Lez, Suze la Rousse, dominated by its magnificent 14th-century castle, has two places where one can taste the wines: the Cave Co-operative la Suzienne and the Château la Borie. South-east, with the greatest registered acreage of vines of any commune in France, is Ste-Cecile-les-Vignes. The village, with its two big *co-operatives*, stands in the wide Aygues valley. It is the acknowledged champion producer of the best of the Côtes du Rhône wines. At the hill village of Cairanne on the left bank of the river is the Cave Co-operative les Coteaux de Cairanne and near by are the ruins of an ancient manastery and a chapel dedicated, perhaps not surprisingly in such a big production wine area as this, to Notre Dame des Exces. The *co-operative* at Cairanne, like that at Ste Cecile, makes a soft and fruity rosé by 'bleeding' the vats 24 hours after the crushed grapes have been pumped into them to ferment.

On the right bank of the Ouveze over to the east, the hill village of Rasteau produces a Côtes du Rhône *rouge* and a *cru reputé*, a strong and naturally sweet wine, excellent served cool as an apéritif with zest of lemon or at room temperature with a dessert. Local people also make a long drink of it with soda. It can be tasted at the *caveau* on the N575 – which runs along the right bank of the Ouveze to Vaison-la-Romaine, a stylish small town set in a luminous landscape which has had a somewhat mobile history. In the early Middle Ages the townsfolk abandoned the Gallo-Roman settlement on the north bank of the Ouveze, building themselves new homes around the 12th-century castle of the counts of Toulouse on the south bank. A few centuries later their descendants re-crossed the river by the Roman bridge still in use to resettle on the north bank, where the modern quarter now is. The two major sights are the well preserved Roman ruins in the Villasse and Puymin quarters on one side of the river, and the ruined château on a spur above the walled medieval *haute ville* on the other. Vaison is proud of its roses, which in this context means not wine but flowers.

A byway off the road that follows the left bank of the Ouveze downstream leads to the small town of Gigondas, once part of the principality of Orange. Dominated by the extraordinary fretted ridge of the 2,410ft Dentelles de Montmirail and topped by a ruined lookout tower, it is a wine name deservedly becoming better known. Its picturesque narrow streets are hemmed in by medieval fortifications and in its ruined castle an open-air theatre is put on in summer. The wines, red, white, and rosé, can be sampled at the *co-operative* or at the cellars of Meffre et Cie. The robust red reminds one of Châteauneuf du Pape, which is not really to be wondered at since as the crow flies the two are a mere ten miles apart.

Like other wines produced in this ruggedly spectacular region, with its mild climate and beautiful vegetation, those of nearby Vacqueyras are very much ones of the warm south. They can be tried at the Caveau des Dentelles de Montmirail, not far from these lace-like rocks.

The D7 running south-east to charmingly named Beaumes de Venise, passes close by the rural Chapel of Notre Dame d'Aubune – a beautiful example of Provençal Romanesque in a remarkable setting. The small mellow town of Beaumes de Venise is built round a delightful Romanesque church at the edge of the Salette river and backed by a cliff pierced by grottoes and crowned by a ruined château. The town is famous for a suave Muscat wine, complete with a glittering golden colour and heady perfume, which can be tasted at the local *caveau*. Delicious when served chilled with ripe melon, it can also be drunk as an apéritif.

West of Beaumes, a byway crosses the Ouveze to join up with the main road leading west to the noisy meridional atmosphere and remarkable Roman monuments of Orange. There is a triumphal arch over 6oft high covered with a wealth of decoration, and a vast theatre built in the reign of Hadrian that was hollowed out of the hill of St Eutrope – its huge flat façade facing the town. The arch is magnificent, despite having been mutilated by the princes of Orange when they transformed it into a fortress in medieval times. Anyone looking at it for the first time might think it strange, as Henry James did, that 'an independent principality in the Middle Ages which fell by marriage into the hands of the family of Nassau should have given its name to the heirs-apparent of the throne of Holland'.

From the top of the steep-sided hill, crowned by a colossal statue of the Virgin, one can look straight down into the theatre. The annual wine fair staged in mid January takes place in the grottoes beneath the theatre, though this is very much an event for professionals.

A minor road leaves the N7 on the southern edge of Orange to pass beneath the Autoroute du Sud and cut across a deserted countryside to

Châteauneuf du Pape. The two chief attractions of this old hill-top town are its views over the Rhône valley and the Mule du Pape restaurant of Père Anselme – happily, one can enjoy both at the same time. As a summer residence of the Avignon popes the town has a long history, owing both its fame and its wine to the papacy.

Although some white wine is made, it is the big dark red – made from a mixture of Bourboulenc, Mourvedre, Cinsault, Pecoui Touar, and Terret Noir grapes – that is famous. The *appellation* it has had since 1935 requires its alcoholic content to be a minimum 12·5°. As a powerful drink with a bouquet that simultaneously suggests truffles and raspberries it may reasonably be called the 'Pope of wines', but, since the pontiffs preferred Burgundy, it is hardly the 'wine of popes' – except in the sense that they encouraged its production.

In the Middle Ages the *vignerons* of the district found it easier, due to the hostility of towns like Lyon and Macon to the north, to export their wine to Italy rather than send it to Paris. The opening of the Canal du Midi in 1680 allowed them to send part of the vintage to England via Bordeaux but in France this state of affairs continued until the edict of 1776 allowed the free circulation of wine.

The Syrah apart, the freestanding vines within the commune are usually pruned to goblet shape. The enormous fist-size stones that cover the vineyards like a pebble beach reflect the sun's rays by day and radiate heat at night. Visitors can taste the wines in the cellars of Clos du Pape, Père Anselme, or Reflets du Châteauneuf.

West of Châteauneuf, on the far side of the Rhône, is Roquemaure with the now-ruined castle where Clement V, the Pope who planted the first vineyards, died in 1314. Roquemaure wines, covered by the Côtes du Rhône *appellation,* can be tasted at the Domaine de St Roch.

South-west is Tavel, set in a rolling landscape cloaked in free-standing vines, long famed for its unusually strong, intensely perfumed, and full-flavoured rosé, slowly dying out because of the exaggerated reverence paid to it. Nearby Lirac also produces a notable rosé, graceful and perfumed, as well as a rare white wine which goes down well with the small game birds that appear on the tables of the restaurants round about. The reds and the rosés are made from Grenache, Cinsault, and Mourvedre, while the white is made mainly from Clairette. To each of these are added grapes of a secondary variety, each grower keeping the exact proportions very much to himself.

Lirac rosés used to be sold under the Tavel *appellation,* but, since 1947 when they were given their own, they have turned to reds with great success. Supple and rounded, they can be tried at the *caveau* in the village.

The list of vineyards on this route along the valley of the Rhône is far from complete, but all journeys must end at some point. Anyone wishing to see more on the return journey might do so by driving to Pont St Esprit on the byways linking up the interesting wine-producing centres and attractive villages of Laudun and Chusclan, each with its tasting cellar and each surrounded by some of the oldest vineyards near the river, despite the apparent newness of their names.

# Provence

Behind the sophisticated coastline of the south of France lies the real Provence, an antique land of great natural beauty, perfumed with wild thyme and lavender, dotted with old *villages perchés* linked by unfrequented serpentine roads, and cloaked in olive groves and vineyards producing agreeable wines that match perfectly the benevolent climate.

The secret life of old Provence is lived in its hill villages, their dark narrow streets ending in squares shaded by venerable plane trees and cooled by ornate fountains, their little *bistrots* serving simple authentic food and local wines in earthenware *pichets*.

Rome was still peopled by barbarians when Phoenician colonists sailed along the coast of Provence 600 years before Christ to found Marseille and plant the first vines on the slopes overlooking an azure-blue sea. The settlers taught the local people how to train and cultivate the vines, to press the grapes, and to make wines from them. Hundreds of years later when Caesar conquered Gaul, he discovered rich vineyards in the region east of Marseille that he named Provincia. Caesar was the first to export the wines to Rome and the first to praise them in his *Commentaries*, declaring them easily the equal of those of Italy and Greece.

Now as then, the wines are light yet full bodied, fruity and well balanced, and best swallowed rather than sipped. Covered since 1956 by the Côtes de Provence VDQS (Vin Delimité de Qualité Superieur) *appellation*, they come in whites and reds as well as the better-known rosés, and are fresh and clean tasting when drunk – which is usually within a year of being made. Their main characteristics are body and warmth, though due to the variety of vines (16 are legally permissible), soils, aspects, and methods of vinification they differ widely in taste. The legal minimum strength is $11°$ for the reds and $11·5°$ for the whites, sometimes made semi-sparkling. Most are bottled by *co-operatives* and individual growers.

The yield from the grapes has quadrupled since the war but is still restricted to 2,000 litres an acre. Since they press only the grapes grown within their own commune, the *co-operatives* make VDQS wines with a more recognizable identity than the blends of the *négociants*. Wines entitled to the *cru classé* distinction are those made from controlled vine varieties with a maximum yield of 1,200 litres an acre. These are choicer vintages, fermented for longer than usual and aged in bottle for at least eighteen months. But even these only have a life of five years at the most.

Many of the wines are made from a multiplicity of grapes, the rosés alone from Cinsault, Grenache, Carignan, and the Pecoui Touar that draws a fruity aroma from arid soils. For red wines the leading grape is the Carignan, but the Tibouren is popular in the Maures massif backing St Tropez, where it produces a delightful bouquet. The Mourvedre, which once covered the whole region, has virtually disappeared. An unusual custom in Provence is to graft several vine varieties onto the same root stock. The stylish white wines are mostly made from Ugni and Clairette grapes.

Most of the vineyards are contained within the *département* or county of the Var, which extends for some 60 miles from Fréjus on the east to Toulon on the west, and reaches north from the sandy beaches of the coast as far as Draguinan and beyond. The summers are dry, rain falling in winter and spring when it falls at all. The sun beats down from a luminous sky for an average of 2,500 hours a year, yet sudden changes of temperature are common. The cold and violent *mistral* wind blows from the north and north-west mostly in spring for an average of 100 days a year, lowering the temperature and drying the atmosphere. If it blows often enough in spring it reduces the risk of mildew on the grapes.

Harvesting takes place at different times, in the Maures in early September and nearer the middle of the month farther north. Poor vintages are unknown, there being only good and better years. *Chaptalisation,* or adding sugar to the must to increase the alcohol content of the wine, is not only forbidden but unnecessary. Fermentation is usually short, four to five days for red wines, a fortnight for whites, and 24 hours for rosés. Some white wine is usually added to the rosés to lower their acidity and accentuate their suppleness.

In the Middle Ages the renown of Provençal wines increased, crude though they must have been compared with present day standards. The Church, through the monasteries, took the grape into its care, its resources and knowledge leading to great advances in viticulture. By the 17th century

A typical September scene.

the reputation of the wines was well established.

The phylloxera disaster struck later in Provence than it did elsewhere, but by the early 1870s the *département* of the Var was completely infected. When the vineyards were replanted, many wine growers – lacking experience and capital – did not always use the best stock, with the result that for some years there was a lowering of the overall quality of the wines. At the turn of the present century a movement began – to plant for quality rather than quantity. The first *co-operatives* in the region were formed in 1905 and multiplied rapidly, leading to more rational and careful vinification and helping many small growers to bring abandoned land into cultivation again. In the same year, the authorities granted a label of quality and estate wines appeared for the first time. Oddly enough, the Allied landings on the beaches west of St Tropez during the last war did much to popularize the wines, and the influx of tourists to the south of France after the war did the rest.

Provençal food and wine taste of the sun-baked land in which they are grown. In this favoured countryside producing four crops of fruit and vegetables a year, olive oil and garlic are the health-giving hallmarks of the pungent and exuberant cuisine. Olive oil replaces butter and cooking fat – and garlic, 'the truffle of Provence', is the true friend of man, as beneficial to digestion as it is to respiration. *Soupe au pistou* is a garlic-flavoured vegetable soup found in nearly every restaurant in spring and autumn but most celebrated of Provençal dishes, eaten with a spoon, is *bouillabaisse*, a savoury fish stew which usually needs to be ordered a day in advance. *Aïoli*, mayonnaise made with olive oil and perfumed with raw garlic, comes with the excellent hors d'oeuvres and *bourride*, a fish soup preferred by many to *bouillabaisse*. It also forms an essential element in *brandade de morue*, in which it is pounded up with salt cod cooked until it is flaky. One of the most delicious fish from the Mediterranean is red mullet, another sea bass, particularly when grilled and flavoured with fennel.

Provençals have a great liking for onions, *pommes d'amour* (tomatoes), courgettes, aubergines, and red and green peppers. Many of these are cooked together in olive oil as *ratatouille*. A savoury local way of preparing artichokes is to flavour them with thyme and stuff them with onions, mushrooms, ham, and salt-pork. The true *salade niçoise* consists of tomatoes, small beans, artichokes, cucumber, green pepper, raw onion, hard-boiled eggs, garlic, fillets of anchovy, and black olives. *Pan bagna* is a slice of bread dipped in olive oil and topped with a miniature *salade niçoise*. *Pissaladière* is an onion tart decorated with anchovy fillets and *pieds et paquets* is lamb tripe stuffed with fat pork, garlic, and parsley. Tournedos steaks are served topped with anchovies, spit-roasted lamb is flavoured with rosemary, and there is wild boar and hare in season along with thrush pâté, a variety of sausages eaten cold, and goats' and ewes' milk cheeses. Fruit ripened by the near-constant sun includes green figs, melons, peaches, apricots, cherries, strawberries, and table grapes.

To cover all the vineyards of the Var on one tour would take more time than most tourists can spare. Better to explore them on one of two circular drives, the first north of the busy N7, which crosses the region from east to west, the second south of it. Both are of necessity over minor roads winding through superbly scenic country on which you rarely meet other cars, even in season. But while it is enjoyable, motoring in this semi-alpine terrain is bound to be slow, a point to bear in mind when calculating distances. The routes of both tours are covered by the yellow Michelin map 84.

Many of the wines of Provence are made at *domaines,* as opulent as châteaux elsewhere but perhaps more difficult to find; most proprietors are glad to give tastings of their wines though some like to be warned in advance. Many of them are in isolated country, and it is usually only the *co-operatives* that one finds in the villages and small towns.

The first tour, mainly around the crystalline massif of the Maures, takes in both the indented coast and the hinterland. It begins at one of Europe's best-known resorts, St Tropez, which takes its name from the Roman magistrate Torpes, put to death for embracing the Christian faith. Before the war it was the haunt of serious artists like Bonnard, Dufy, Matisse, and Utrillo. That was before it was adopted by the dilettantes of the French film set. Some of the works of the first group, if none of the second, can be found in the Musée de l'Annonciade, containing the finest collection of modern paintings in France. The resort faces north, turning its back on the three fine beaches a mile or so away to the west, on the other side of the headland. The inhabitants originally came from Genoa (60 families were settled there after the small town was razed to the ground in 1470), proved by the names on the graves in the cemetery on the headland. Among the more interesting sights in St Tropez are the Château de Suffren, the Misericorde Chapel, the old prisons, and the ramparts and towers.

It is often forgotten that St Tropez is a fishing port, makes ships, and catches tunny and anchovies. The citizens once had the right to form their own army and navy and the faded uniforms are brought out for the Bravade in mid May – a date which commemorates the defence of the town against the Spanish fleet in 1637. The way west is on the N98A, turning left to go inland and climb in *lacets* up to Gassin, a *village perché* with its houses packed together within the ancient ramparts overlooking the bay of St Tropez. You can 'take the air' on the Sénéquier terrace above the vineyards planted with Tibouren, an ancient Provençal vine variety. On the way to Ramatuelle the road passes the superb property of Château Minuty, the

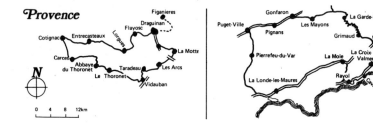

vines surrounding it producing red and rosé wines as well as a Blanc de Blancs. On the same road and well worth calling at for a tasting is the Domaine de Restaud. Near by, too, is the *co-operative* formed in 1964 by the Maitres Vignerons de la Presqu'île de St Tropez, each of whom sends his best *cuvée* there for vinification.

Ramatuelle, a picturesque market town in the centre of the headland at an altitude of nearly 1,700ft, is crowned by a castle near which is the cemetery where young girls still put flowers on the grave of the French film star Gerard Philippe. The small town is noted for its wine and is the place where the local people come to sit on the terrace of the Café de l'Ormeau, shaded by a majestic 17th-century elm tree. The wines can be sampled at the Domaine Bastide Blanche and the local *co-operative*.

The road winds down in continuous hairpins over the easy Col de Collebasse to Croix Valmer, a resort a mile or two from the sea in a wooded setting. Near the village is the Domaine de la Croix, with one of the oldest vineyards in Provence. The stone cross on the summit of the nearby Col de la Croix recalls the legend that the Emperor Constantine on his way to Rome saw in the sky a cross engraved *in hoc signo vinces* (by this sign will you conquer), an accurate prediction as it turned out.

The N559 skirts the bay of Cavalaire, protected from the *mistral* by the Pradel chain of mountains, to reach Cavalaire, a lively resort with a long sandy beach where Allied troops landed in August 1944. The local wine, La Croix de Cavalaire, is well known. Forming part of the beautiful Corniche des Maures, the road continues along the coast to Le Rayol, an elegant resort terraced above the sea in a sheltered situation, and La Canadel, where the Saracen raids that were the scourge of this coast until put down by the Foreign Legion were re-enacted in August 1944 by more pro than anti Moroccan troops serving in the French army. Beyond Le Canadel a right turn onto the D27 leads inland over the Col du Canadel, its summit little higher than 845ft yet commanding immense views of the Maures mountains and the coast. A left turn onto the N98 leads to La Mole and through the Forêt du Dom to La Londe des Maures, in the Pansard valley, where the tasting cellars of the *domaines* of Galoupet, La Source Ste Marguerite, and Cheylanne can be visited.

Beyond the Domaine de Mauvanne, noted for its wines, the scenic D12 forks right to go inland to Pierrefeu, in a picturesque situation on a promontory in the valley of Réal Martin. In the village is a *co-operative* and the Domaine de la Tour Ste Anne and east on the D14 to Collobrières is the Domaine de Montaud. The nearby small town of Puget Ville has the important wine-producing Domaine du Mas. From here the N97 goes north-east to Pignans, a wine village in a setting of cork-tree woods. South-east off the road through the forest is the superb viewpoint of Notre Dame des Anges, 2,505ft up. On the way is the Domaine de Rimauresq, owned by the same family of *vignerons* for 300 years.

Next comes Gonfaron, curiously built round a knoll, and known among Provençals for its legend of the flying asses. East off the road to Les Mayons is the Domaine de la Tuilière, famed for its mellow red wines. Beyond

Les Mayons, washed by the Réal Martin, the Aille, and other streams, is La Garde Freinet, an old village at an altitude of 1170ft dominating the rich plain of Argens. One of its main activities is making bottle corks from the cork oaks in the nearby forests. Dominating the village is a ruined fortress where the Saracens remained entrenched for nearly 250 years, pillaging the surrounding area. A worthwhile excursion from La Garde Freinet is to Plan de la Tour, a hill village hanging on the side of the mountain, with vast views of the bay of St Tropez from its vineyards. The scenic road winds south to Grimaud, a village terraced beneath its ruined château and one of the warmest places along the coast in winter. Among its old arcaded houses is a Romanesque church which adjoins what is said to have been the 'house of the Templars'. From Grimaud it is an easy drive south-east back to St Tropez.

The second tour begins at Draguinan, the chief town of the Var spread out on a plateau at the foot of the Malmot mountain, its wide straight streets full of bustle on market day. The old town is isolated on a knoll crowned by a 17th-century clock tower; among the picturesque medieval streets is the Romanesque façade of a 13th-century synagogue and the ancient palace of the bishops of Fréjus housing an interesting museum and library. From Draguinan, a classic excursion is to the tiny hill village of Figanières, reached by a turning off the road to Grasse near the roadside Chapel of St Pons. The village is noted for its silkworm culture and the wines that can be tasted at its *co-operative*.

From Draguinan the route heads west for Flayosc, a typical Provençal village on a feudal mound 1,035ft high, with 14th-century fortified gates, a ruined château, and a church with a Romanesque nave. The *vin rouge* of Flayosc is deservedly popular hereabouts. A picturesque road winds over the forested hills to the small town of Lorgues, an eagle's nest if ever there was one, typically Provençal, centred on a beautiful main square shaded by plane trees and cooled by the waters of a monumental fountain. A drive a few miles east on the N562 brings you to Castel Roubine, a *domaine* producing a notable white wine. A byway passing near St Antonin leads to the pretty village of Entrecasteaux, and, a few miles on, Cotignac, at the foot of a 260ft-high cliff topped by two 15th-century round towers and burrowed into at the base by grottoes. Charming old houses surround the picturesque *place de l'hôtel de ville*, with its ancient fountain. A steep climb south-west of the village takes you to Mont Verdaille and the Chapel of Notre Dame de Grace, built in 1519, where Anne of Austria came to pray for a son and was rewarded nine months later when she gave birth to the child who was to become Louis XIV. Off the D13/D22 to the south is the Domaine de Nestuby, where one can taste the white wines grown on the Côte de Mont Bessillon, one source of the truffles served at restaurants in the district.

Continuing on the D13 brings one to the small town of Carces, with its *co-operative* Vinicole la Carçoise which binds together 300 *vignerons* and 500 hectares of vineyards. South of the town in a forested setting is the artificial lake of Carces, with the Grande Ecluse waterfall at its western edge.

Another worthwhile excursion from the town is west to Montfort, near the *cascade* or waterfall of the Grand Baou and, farther on, the village of Correns, famed for its white wine and its medieval *pardon,* in a pretty setting in the valley of the Argens.

From Carces the route goes east on the N562 to follow the Argens before turning off for the Abbey of Thoronet, built of the local red stone and situated in a valley shaded by cypress trees. The Provençal Romanesque church of the Abbey, consecrated in 1147 by St Bernard, conforms to the Cistercian rule, of austerity, its vaulted nave supported by five pillars. As well as the oratory, with its magnificent acoustics, one can see the underground sacristy, the abbot's quarters, and an austere Romanesque cloister on two levels. In the vaulted cellar are ancient casks and a wine press. There could hardly be a better reminder of Pope's lines 'happy convents, bosomed deep in vines, where slumber abbots, purple as their wines'.

From the Abbey, a delightfully scenic byway follows the Argens east to the town of Vidauban – partly enclosed in a loop of the river. Here there are many places where one can taste the wines: the *co-operative* makes a Blanc de Blancs, the Domaine de Matheron some smooth red wines, and the *négociant* Bernard produces the famed Bouquet de Provence rosé. To the south, on the D48 to La Garde Freinet, is the Domaine des Esperifets and the Domaine de Peissonnel.

A byway leads north from Vidauban to Taradeau, passing close by the Château St Martin, a former priory, the vineyards that surround it famous in the 12th century. They make white, rosé, and red wines. A *cru classé,* the *domaine* is owned by the Comte de Rohan Chabot, a leading figure in the promotion of Côtes de Provence wines. The picturesque village of Taradeau is also famous for its dry white wines and full-bodied reds, which can be sampled at the local *co-operative.*

Les Arcs sur Argens, on the east, is a notable market for local wines. It surrounds a castle where a popular Provençal saint, Ste Roseline, was born in 1250. To the east, beside the D91 to La Motte, is the Château Roseline, set in a park decorated with fountains. The Château was once the ancient Abbey of La Celle Roubaud, first mentioned in the local archives of 1038, and has borne since 1505 the name of the priory patronised by Pope John XXII who created the vineyards that surround it. In the vaulted chapel are priceless works of art: 15th-century paintings on wood, a reredos, and carved Renaissance choir-stalls.

On the D25 to the east of La Motte the Seda establishment makes the well-known Les Demoiselles rosé, popular in England. The way back to Draguinan is by Trans-en-Provence, an old hill town famed for its Nartuby waterfalls.

The wines of Provence may never match the *grands crus* in prestige, but, while their fragrant bouquet reminds the drinker of the gay sunny land where the troubadours sang at courts of love, they are certain to keep their popular appeal.

# Armagnac

Rivers fanning out north from the Pyrenees give a clue to the lie of the land in brandy-producing Armagnac, the heart of ancient Gascony. Centred on the Baise, it is bounded on the east by the Gers (the name chosen for the *département* created at the Revolution that replaced most of the former province), and on the west by the Arros and the Adour. The long ridges or lines of hills between these valleys make life all ups and downs for travellers going east-west, plain sailing for those going north-south.

In 1909 the boundaries of the region entitled to the Armagnac *appellation* were marked out: Haut Armagnac in the east, Tenareze in the centre, and Bas Armagnac, most highly prized, in the west. Auch is the main centre for Haut Armagnac, Condom for Tenareze, and Eauze for Bas Armagnac. Two of these sub-divisions spill out beyond the *département* of the Gers: part of Bas Armagnac juts into the Landes and the Tenareze extends north beyond Nerac, in the Lot et Garonne.

With a darker hue and a more pungent aroma, armagnac is the only brandy that can claim to be as good as Cognac. As good as, certainly, but quite different. The rule about warming a glass of Cognac in the hand and sniffing the bouquet before tasting it needs to be followed even more closely when the *ballon* is filled with armagnac. An unwashed empty glass that has contained the brandy will give off its scent for days, and the buyers of armagnac who congregate in the main square of the small market-town of Eauze rarely need to taste it. They simply pour a little of the spirit into the palms of their hands, rub them together, and inhale. In this way they claim not only to know which part of the region it came from but also how old it is.

But this traditional method of marketing shows how armagnac suffers in comparison with Cognac, in that it is not sold by financially powerful shippers who by publicising their own brand make the product itself better known. Isolated within the triangle Bordeaux-Toulouse-Bayonne and bypassed by main waterways and roads, Armagnac is a unique haven for those who seek the unspoiled charm of *la vieille France* but is badly placed when it comes to getting its brandy as widely appreciated as it ought to be. Cognac has been recognised in Britain for centuries, but there was no mention of armagnac in the Oxford English Dictionary until 1910.

Like any other brandy, armagnac is distilled from white wine by boiling it and cooling the vapour it gives off to convert the concentrate back into liquid. Here, as in Cognac, the wine is inferior – thin, acidic, and low in alcohol. Since it may not by law be racked or filtered beforehand, distillation starts as soon as the fermented must has cooled down. The wine is heated in an old-fashioned pot still, which can only treat one batch at a time but preserves more of the inherent flavours. Only one distillation is the tradition, not two as in Cognac, and it is carried on at a lower temperature, leaving the still at 50° alcohol. But the fashion is growing to distil the liquid twice so that the spirit matures earlier, which is a pity as this removes some of the elements that make armagnac what it is.

Armagnac is aged in casks made of the local black oak, dark and so full of sap that it can only be sawn and shaped with an adze. This gives the brandy its dark colour and racy flavour, and helps it age more quickly. No armagnac may be sold until it has been matured for two years, though in fact three-star armagnac will have been aged for three or four years and a VSOP for anything from five to twelve. When bottled, the brandy must have an alcoholic strength of 40°.

The technique of distilling wine into alcohol was introduced into Gascony by the Moors from Spain who overran south-west France in the 8th century. The word used in Armagnac for a pot still, *alambic*, is of Arabic origin. In the 16th century distillation was really under way in the region and by 1650 an important trade existed in *eaux de vie* or water of life, a term coined in earlier times by the alchemists who had guarded the secret for so long.

In 1666 there were as many as 60 stills in Armagnac, each distilling 100 barrels of wine a day. By 1700 *bouilleurs ambulants* had appeared. These were freelance distillers using mobile stills, looking like antique steam-engines and drawn by oxen, a few of which operate in the region even now. Distillation being mainly a peasant activity and costing little more than the wood for the furnace, armagnac was sold in those days for much the same price as wine. At one time over 100 mobile stills were circulating in Armagnac, going from one farmhouse to another, the men operating them being welcomed back each year like old friends. Hornbeam and oak were the woods traditionally used to heat the still, the first for its flame, the second for its long-lasting embers.

Rural distillation developed in this way because in the reign of Louis XI the wine growers of Bordeaux won the right to block exports of wines from nearby regions until November 11, a date by which ships from northern countries had returned to their home ports for the winter. Bordeaux being the only feasible port for the export of armagnac, the blockade was complete. Since spirit uses fewer barrels than wine and is easier to keep, the Gascons were forced to turn to distilling if they were to earn any money from their vines.

After the phylloxera disaster in 1875 the vineyards were replanted and early this century the region was awarded its *appellation* and its boundaries defined. The three regions contained within them form a plateau sloping to the west. Its geological character varies from limestone to ochre-coloured clay, the acid topsoil being more sandy on the west. Rain and hail-storms are common in spring but the long dry summer is followed by a beautifully soft autumn. The winter is mild, really cold weather is rare, and snow unknown. The predominant vine variety is Ugni Blanc though Picpoul (or Piquepoult), Folle Blanche, Colombard, and Clairette are also popular.

Up to the Revolution not a lot of armagnac was exported, though the American War of Independence in 1777 gave an unexpected boost to overseas demand when the colonies in revolt boycotted any spirits sent out from England. Two traditional routes by which armagnac was taken to the Atlantic coastal ports of Bordeaux and Bayonne were the rivers Adour and Garonne, but road and rail have made both redundant. Oddly enough, it was the export of the brandy that gave it its name, first used at the ports to distinguish it from those of Languedoc and the Charente.

For the Gascons, genuinely attached to old ways, armagnac – the product of three civilisations (made of Gascon wine, distilled in an alambic invented by the Arabs, and matured in oak barrels devised by the ancient Gauls) – is one of their basic traditions. Gascon knights are said to have gone to the Crusades with two keys: one to their wives' chastity belts, the other to their wine cellars. In the guide he wrote for pilgrims setting out in the 12th century on the long and dangerous walk across France to the shrine of Santiago de Compostella in northern Spain, the monk Aymer Picard told them that in Gascony they would find tasty white bread and good red wine but also talkative, cynical people who drank heavily. 'Even so', he added, 'the Gascons fight well and are kind to the poor.' This squares with our image of them as swashbuckling adventurers who had the good sense to do their fighting on other people's territory, like those who battled against the English on the side of Joan of Arc. Immortalized by Dumas, their archetype is d'Artagnan, captain of the king's *mousquetaires,* always ready to draw his sword, fond of talk in good company, and with an inborn love of eating and drinking well. Except that they are no more belligerent than the next man, present-day Gascons fit this picture perfectly. For proof of this consider their cuisine, rich, varied, and plentiful, with many of the dishes still prepared in the original manner. Here, where not one but two meat courses are the rule, most meals start with a thick *garbure,* a soup made of cabbage, ham, bacon, and preserved goose. Alternatives are garlic ('drunkard's') soup or chicken *bouillon* resulting from a *poule au pot* such as the Gascon Henri IV wanted every family in his kingdom to enjoy on Sundays. Next might come an assortment of cold sausages or grilled slices of black *boudin* served hot with toast.

In Armagnac, chicken tastes as chicken should but duck and goose are the more common entries on restaurant menus. More of these birds are reared for the table than in any other part of France. The livers of both are prized, and, served with country style bread in numerous ways (uncooked, cooked with or without garlic, with quails' eggs in a *cocotte,* or plainly poached) are obligatory. At Christmas-time, Gascon farmers send mature turkeys to Paris by the thousand but they themselves prefer the more tender ones of summer. One delicious way they prepare them is as *ballotine de dinde à la toulousaine,* boned, but with the skin left intact, then stuffed with a forcemeat of sweetbreads and mushrooms – the whole thing is then poached. Fresh-water fish such as pike, trout, lamprey, and – in the west in season – salmon are cooked in interesting ways. Game is nowhere more abundant: it ranges from *palombe* (wood pigeon), *caille* (quail), and *faisan* (pheasant) to *perdreaux* (young partridge), though so far as small game birds go, *ortolan* and *bécasse* (woodcock) are easily the most popular. When Louis XIV passed through Armagnac on the way to meet his future bride, the infant Marie Thérèse, at the Franco-Spanish frontier, d'Artagnan offered him a typical peasant dish: quail rolled in oiled vine leaves and grilled over a fire of vine shoots. It is still a dish native to the region. So is casserole of quails cooked in freshly pressed grape juice and *ragoût* of woodcock. The liver of goose and duck is cooked in its natural state and served with grapes, while the meat is made into *galantines* or preserved in its own fat as a *confit*. Called by its Gascon name *lou magret*, breast of duck is prepared in a special way by the great chefs of the region like Daguin of Auch and Sandrini of Condom. Like other restaurateurs, they pride themselves on the traditional dishes of stuffed breast of veal and *cassoulet,* usually made with only one kind of meat and therefore less rich than the Toulouse version.

Beef is excellent, particularly as steak or *estouffat*, cooked in a casserole resting on belly of pork and covered with a *mirepoix* of onions, shallots, and carrots. Pork may be cooked in a similar way. Lamb is good, too, particularly leg roasted on a spit as *gigot à la ficelle.*

One or two of the cheeses are interesting, like the goats' cheese *à l'armagnac*, but the Gascons are not great cheese eaters and prefer sweet things like *croustade*, a pie made of apples marinated in armagnac, *glace aux pruneaux* or ice cream mixed with shredded prunes treated in the same way, and flans encasing luscious fruit: pears, peaches, or apricots. Among the *patisseries* is *pastis*, not an aniseed flavoured drink but flaky pastry enclosing orange flowers. Neither the flowers nor the fruit of oranges is hard to come by, for the trees ripen in almost every garden.

Most meals end with brandy – every restaurant has its collection of *vieux* armagnacs – though the spirit makes its pungent presence known in most courses and sometimes, as newly made armagnac blanc, between them. The 'good wyn of Gaskoyne' known and liked in medieval England may now be a thing of the past but drinkable wines are still made in Armagnac. Some too good for distilling are Madiran, Pacherenc, Côtes de Montestruc, and Montréal, which come both red and white. One of the locally made sparkling wines is made from the vineyards of the Château of Monluc.

A popular hero still, the cavalier-type figure of d'Artagnan – with wide brimmed hat and high floppy boots – appears on bottles of armagnac; phrases associated with him like *pousse rapière* and *coup de foudre* are used as names for popular variations on *le cocktail* – the basis of which consists of a measure of armagnac in a tall glass topped up with a sparkling white wine of the region. They are refreshing, though deceptively potent.

Apart from the work that goes on in the vineyards and the distilleries, about the only 'industry' is mixed farming – astonishing as it may seem, there are a total of three sets of traffic lights in the whole of the *département*. As all the towns are small and built to human scale, so most roads are happily free from traffic. The landscape, cut into original relief by the rivers, is gently undulating for the most part, with views from the higher ground of the backdrop of the Pyrénées, 60-odd miles to the south. The yellow Michelin maps 79 and 82 cover the region. What follows is a suggested circular tour within the area covered by the Armagnac *appellation*, starting in the north in the Lot et Garonne. There are ample opportunities for tasting the brandy along the way.

At the turn of the century barges laden with barrels of armagnac destined for ships waiting at Bordeaux passed through the sleepy small town of

Nérac, cut in two by the Baise. Petit Nérac, on the right bank, with 16th-century houses lining its steep winding streets, still has a medieval air. Time was, too, when Grand Nérac, across the hump-backed bridge on the left bank, was the scene of a brilliant court when Marguerite, daughter of Catherine de Médicis and Queen of Navarre, lived and loved surrounded by poets and philosophers. The only reminder of this period is a wing of the 15th-century stronghold of the princes of Béarn (now housing the municipal museum), and a statue of Henri IV – *noustré Henric* in Gascon – in the Allées d'Albret, the route taken by southbound traffic. Nérac is still a centre for armagnac, which can be tasted at the Pallas cellars. Along the river bank to the south is the beautiful promenade de la Garenne, dotted with fountains.

Jutting out like the prow of a ship above the pretty Auzoue valley south-west of Nérac is Montréal, a *bastide* or town built for defence in 1289. Though it was sacked by Montgomery during the crusade against the Albigensian heresy it retains the characteristic grid pattern of streets and an arcaded central square with adjoining Gothic church. The need for towns of this kind arose because from the mid-12th century to the mid-15th century Gascony formed the eastern border of the Plantagenet-controlled Guyenne and was systematically pillaged by the Duke of Lancaster and his successors. Over 70 towns of this kind exist in Armagnac.

A pretty road runs west from Montréal to Castelnau, which takes its Gascon name from the 'new' castle on the hill round which its houses are built. The Church of Notre Dame de Pibèque is the scene of a local pilgrimage several times a year. West again is Barbotan-les-Thermes, an attractive small spa in a wooded valley whose sulphur and radioactive waters are said to be an antidote to rheumatism. Curiously placed at the entrance

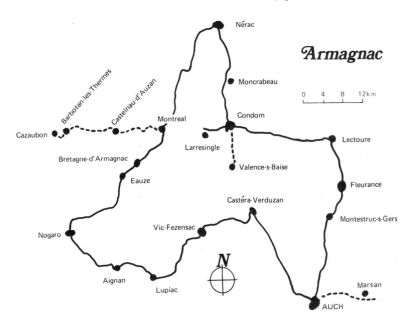

to the thermal park is a 12th-century church with a belfry wall that was once a fortified gate set in the ramparts. A ruined castle dominates the town, surrounded by some of the best vineyards in Bas Armagnac. The vine-covered slopes giving wide views around nearby Cazaubon, too, produce a locally renowned armagnac and in season the village has a *stand de degustation* or tasting bar operated by the chain of *co-operatives* entitled Union des Caves de Vinification de l'Armagnac or UCVA for short. Bretagne d'Armagnac, on the road south from Montréal, adjoins a trinity of attractive boating lakes with the weird names of Zou-Fou-Dou.

The sleepy small town of Eauze, the ancient Elusa of the Romans, is the main marketing centre for the brandies of Bas Armagnac, some of which can be sampled at the premises of Sica Armagnaçaise. While there, one can also see how distilling 100 litres of wine of 10° alcohol makes 20 litres of *eaux de vie* at 50° – a simple five to one reduction. Market-day in Eauze is the scene of much informal buying and selling of the spirit around the Café de France near the brick-built church.

Nogaro, south-west of Eauze, is an elongated small town founded in 1060, typical of the *sauvetés* which here preceded the *bastides*. The Romancsque St Austinde Church, one of the largest in the Gers and one of the most beautiful, is entered by a porch topped by a portal depicting Christ-in-majesty flanked by the four Evangelists. The sombre interior, with its round columns and nave of three bays, adjoins a Romanesque cloister. At the nearby village of Laujuzan are the tasting cellars of the hospitable Samalens family, *négociants en armagnac de père et fils*.

South-east is another *bastide,* that of Aignan, perched on a crest ringed by wooded hills. Sacked by the Black Prince operating from Bordeaux in 1355, the town had like all others in Gascony to pay homage to him five years later when the treaty of Bretigny gave the whole of south-west France to the English. Armagnacs of various ages, along with prunes, chestnuts, green-gages, and other fruits macerated in the spirit, can be tried at the well-known Maison Sempé. An enjoyable drive from Aignan takes one south-west to Termes d'Armagnac, on the perimeter of the ancient province. The castle keep is one of the highest in the region; from the top, reached by a spiral staircase of 150 steps, there are fine views of the valleys of the Arros and the Adour. Adjoining the parish church, the keep houses the Musée de Panache, with exhibits that relate this admirable characteristic to the military-history of Gascony.

In a pretty setting east of Aignan, Lupiac is the best point from which to approach the Château of Castelmore, birthplace in 1615 of Charles de Batz – better known as d'Artagnan – who left his homeland to seek his fortune in Paris, became the confidant of Louis XIV, and died at the siege of Maastricht in 1673.

East again is Vic Fezensac, the most lively town in the region, particularly on one of its many fête days. The *course landaise* that takes place then is less a bullfight, more a test of agility in which the participant least likely to get hurt is the bull. With a Romanesque church containing interesting furniture, the town is a noted centre of gastronomy and the base of several

A course landaise: an economy bullfight where the bull is always spared.

armagnac shippers, one of whom operating from the Château Notre Dame markets the grandly titled Armagnac des Gourmets.

On the road to Castura Verduzan is the Château de Bonas, where the Marquis of that name, while under house arrest during the Terror, made the first attempt to rationalise the production of armagnac. The ancillary buildings are well enough preserved to show the ingenious methods he adopted, one of which was to use gravity and the natural slope of the ground to methodically transform grapes into wine and the wine into brandy. He also substituted the single for the double distillation which later inspired Edouard Adam to produce a revolutionary alambic for this purpose – in which the vapour before condensing is passed through pipes cooled by the wine waiting to be distilled. This is now the only permitted method.

Beyond the Baise river is Auch, the administrative capital of Gascony until the Revolution, and an attractive small town on a steep hill above the Gers. It was once an important halt for pilgrims from the Languedoc, Provence, and Italy on the way to Santiago de Compostella in Spain. Above a monumental stairway climbing up from the river, overlooked at the halfway mark by a statue of d'Artagnan, is the magnificent Cathedral of Ste Marie. The Renaissance décor of its west façade leaves one unprepared for the severity of its Gothic interior, although it is lit by some of the most significant stained-glass windows in the world. Renowned throughout France, the 113 choir-stalls are four centuries old and depict in lifelike carvings as many as 1,500 people, some sectarian, some religious. No one should leave Auch without spending some time in the building. Nor, since Auch is the main centre for Haut Armagnac, should he miss calling at the Maison de l'Armagnac in the Rue Gambetta.

A worthwhile drive east from Auch takes you to the Château de Marsan, the ancestral home of the Montesquieu family, whose roots go deep in Gascony. The Château is fronted by a formal garden and adjoins the Chapel of St Martin housing the ancestral tombs.

The next part of the route follows the Gers river as it flows north through the towns of Fleurance and Lectoure to mark the eastern boundary of the Armagnac *appellation*. A curious feature of the river, common to all those flowing north through the region, is the lack of symmetry between one side of the valley and the other, the slope of the right bank being much steeper than the left. In a beautiful setting near the road about five miles north of Auch is the Château of Rieutort, one-time home of the Comte du Barry – husband of the famous countess – who sold his wife to the king. Five miles on is Montestruc, where the SICA *co-operative* produces a fair quantity of drinkable red wine. Haut Armagnac produces more red wine than white, in fact, and only in good years is the second distilled into brandy.

Fleurance is another *bastide* built in 1280 by the Cistercian monks of the Abbey of Bouillac, now a lonely ruin to the north-west. The delightfully named town is centred on a beautiful 14th-century church and an arcaded central square. Near by is a magnificent round medieval *halle* or covered market. To the north, on a spur 300ft above the Gers, Lectoure is still ringed by its medieval ramparts. Built on the foundations of a Roman settlement, it was from 1324 the capital of Armagnac until this was joined to the French crown in 1487. Among the many fascinating old buildings is the ruined castle of the counts of Armagnac and the severely styled Church of St Gervais-St Protais. The rebuilding of the choir of the Church in the 16th century led to the discovery of several 2nd-4th-century pagan altars, now in the town museum. From the Promenade du Bastion near the castle there are wide views of the Pyrénées. In the Rue Montebello is the house where Marshal Lannes was born in 1769. 'I found him a pygmy and made him a giant', Napoleon said of him, which was unjust, for, like a true Gascon, Lannes – made Duke of Montebello by the Emperor – was a formidable fighter and made his own reputation by the battles he won.

Reached by a scenic road winding west from Lectoure, Condom was a commercial centre for armagnac from the earliest times and still has the biggest stocks of the brandy. The town became an important river port when the Baise river was canalised in the mid-19th century. Armagnac is no longer transported by water but the *chais* overlooking the quays between the two bridges across the river are still in use. Atop the narrow paved streets of the old quarter is the forbidding Cathedral of St Pierre. It was built in 1506 on the site of an ancient monastery, with a single luminous nave flanked by lateral chapels between the buttresses. Inside the adjoining town hall is a 16th-century cloister with Gothic arcades above which is the Musée d'Armagnac devoted to the making of the brandy, now bottled in mass-produced flagons called *basquaises*. Until the 19th century the bottles were of all shapes and sizes, made by hand in small workshops dotted about the countryside – wherever sand for glass making and wood for the furnace were to hand. One specimen on view in the museum is the Dame Jeanne, found at Aignan, which holds 18 litres.

In one of the narrow streets off the Place Bossuet near the Cathedral is the house that once belonged to Blaise de Monluc, called the 'royal butcher' by the Protestants he so ruthlessly hounded in the 16th century. Badly dis-figured in battle, he was forced to wear a mask to the end of his days.

East of Condom is the fortified Abbey of La Romieu, the outline of some of its pentagon-shaped fortifications still visible. The Abbey, at its most powerful in the 11th century, was a halt for pilgrims on the way to the shrine of Santiago in Spain.

Off the Montréal road a few miles west of Condom is the imposing *bastide* of Larresingle enclosed by deep moats and high walls and entered by fortified gates. Alongside the ruined château within the walls is its ancient chapel, now the parish church.

South of Condom, along a pretty road beside the Baïse, Valence is another *bastide* built on a promontory to a regular plan around a central arcaded square. Contrary to medieval tradition, which authorised only one belfry to a parish, the church in the square has two rising up above its Romanesque façade.

But there is nothing at Valence to compare with the ancient Cistercian Abbey of Flaran, north-west of the town. One of the finest examples of the style of architecture adopted by the Order, the church has a barrel-vaulted nave and adjoins an early-14th-century colonnaded cloister. Noteworthy among the well-preserved group of buildings is the *chais* where the monks stored their wine. Dominating the village of Beaucaire, a few miles south of Valence, are the immense ruins of the Château of Pardaillan, seat of one of the most important baronies in all Gascony, bristling with towers and high walls. One of the last barons had the misfortune to be the husband of the infamous Comtesse de Parabère, mistress of Louis XV.

Moncrabeau, a village in the true Gascon tradition off the road north to Nérac, is renowned for its Academy of Liars. The initiation of new members takes place in front of the 'chair of truth' embedded in the wall of the church.

# Bordelais

More fine wines come from the rolling and softly coloured countryside around Bordeaux than anywhere else on earth. The region is also tops for quantity, producing some 500 million bottles of wine a year. Covering virtually the whole of the big *département* or county of the Gironde, about 100 miles across, are 250,000 acres of vines inset with over 3,000 châteaux. Built mostly in the 18th century by the rich merchants of Bordeaux, these are not so much castles as 'places in the country'. But since it is in them that the finest vintages are made and can be tasted, they are obviously important halts on any pilgrimage to this mecca of good taste.

Dominating the Bordelais, as the region is called, are the rivers Garonne and Dordogne, which join up near Bordeaux and continue flowing north-west to enter the Bay of Biscay as the Gironde. Along the right bank of the combined river are the lesser vineyards of Bourg and Blaye, but at the eastern edge of the triangular-shaped Medoc on the left bank are the highest quality vineyards of all. Below Bordeaux, along the left bank of the Garonne, the Medoc is continued on the south-east by the Graves district enclosing at its southern end the small areas of Cérons and Sauternes. Between the right bank of the Garonne and the left bank of the Dordogne is the vast white wine country of Entre deux Mers, at the edge of which is the narrow band of Premiers Côtes de Bordeaux vineyards. North of the Dordogne around Libourne are the red wine areas of Castillon, St Emilion, Pomerol, and Fronsac, and backing these and the Côtes of Bourg and Blaye on the north-west are extensive vineyards covered by the generic *appellation* Bordeaux. Here as elsewhere in the region, this embraces red and white wines (some made *mousseux* or sparkling) as well as *clairets* or rosés. Next come Bordeaux Supérieur followed by named districts such as Graves and finally, at the top of the ladder, the named vineyards of the châteaux.

Whereas the wines of Burgundy take the name of the province where they are grown, those of the Gironde are known as bordeaux, a measure of the way the city has dominated the region since it was occupied by the English in the early Middle Ages. At the beginning of the 18th century, the only wines highly thought of in Paris were Champagne, Burgundy, and a few lesser *crus* produced near the capital. Almost all the bordeaux then being made was sent to England, as it had been for centuries. Nowadays, the biggest buyer of Bordelais wines is Belgium, with Britain coming fourth after West Germany and the United States.

Here, as in other parts of France, viticulture was at first an ecclesiastic and an urban activity, and even now the delimited area of Graves extends to the outer fringes of Bordeaux. In Burgundy, one wine is usually made from one variety of grape but in the Bordelais several varieties are used. For the great whites the trinity of Sauvignon, Semillon, and Muscadelle is traditional; for the reds it is Merlot, Cabernet, and Malbec. From the religious orders the vineyards passed into the hands of the feudal barons, some later being taken over by well-to-do merchants. After the Revolution the vineyards of the

dispossessed aristocracy were bought mainly by people seeking an invest-
ment, and many are now owned by private and public companies.

Even more than Burgundy, red bordeaux needs time. On the Atlantic side
of France the grapes ripen later than they do in Burgundy, and the skins and
juice are fermented together for at least ten days instead of the Burgundian
seven. Sometimes the wine remains in cask for two or three years before
being bottled, and never less than eighteen months, whereas most
Burgundies are bottled after a year. No first-growth claret is ready for
drinking until it has been about seven years in bottle, though it will continue
to develop for a long time after that.

Away from Bordeaux and the N10 through-route either side of it, the
modest hotels are used more by French bagmen than British tourists. At
these, the table is more reliable than the plumbing. For honest food elsewhere, avoiding popular and pricey places like St Emilion, one should seek
out those restaurants off the beaten track that are patronized by the locals.
Food of the Bordelais is classical French, with not a trace of an English
accent despite this having been an *ancien dominion britannique*. The variety
of fish dishes is unending, from the oysters of the nearby Marennes or
Arcachon basin and the mussels, prawns, and shrimps of the coast to the
*lamproie* or lamprey and caviar of the Gironde – as good as the Russian and
as dear. Salmon and *alose* or shad also come from the Gironde. Dishes
labelled *à la bordelaise* means that they come garnished with a sauce made
of claret, tomato, butter, shallots, thyme, nutmeg, and seasoning: in this
category are entrecôte and tournedos steaks, *cèpes* or mushrooms, and fish
such as lamprey and sole. The lamb of Pauillac in the Medoc is outstanding.
Quail and rabbit are cooked in white wine. There are succulent asparagus
and other early vegetables from the marshes, salads dressed in walnut oil,
cheeses aged in red wine, and delicious prunes, peaches, and strawberries
from the Garonne valley. Blaye is famed for its *pralines* or crisp almond
cakes, St Emilion for its macaroons.

Motoring in the Bordelais is uncomplicated: there are no hills to speak of,
most towns are small, and roads generally carry little traffic. The suggested
tour through the vineyards encircles Bordeaux in an anti-clockwise direction
but avoids the city itself, with its hopelessly disorganised road layout and
tangled traffic. The route begins and ends at Blaye, on the right bank of the
Gironde north of Bordeaux, crosses the river by ferry, then passes through
the Medoc and the districts of Graves and Entre deux Mers before crossing
over to the right bank of the Dordogne to take in Castillon, St Emilion,
Fronsac, and Bourg on the way back to Blaye. The three yellow Michelin
maps 71, 75, and 79 cover the region.

Many châteaux proprietors put visiting on a rather formal basis, asking
for two days advance notice. If you feel that this conflicts with the freedom
of touring you should call instead at the more immediately welcoming
*caves co-operatives*.

At an ancient crossing of the Gironde, the agreeable small town of Blaye is
dominated by the huge walled and moated citadel built in 1689 by Vauban
on a mound once topped by a Roman encampment. From the fortress –

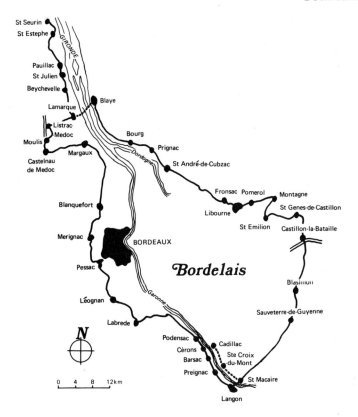

where the Duchesse de Berry, widowed at the age of 12, was imprisoned in 1832 – there are fine views of the river and its islands. The vineyards backing the town produce wines of middling quality and are covered by the generic *appellations* Blaye and Côtes de Blaye. From the port, a car ferry and naviplane cross the Gironde at intervals to Lamarque, a small town built round its 12th-century castle in the very centre of the Medoc – the triangular peninsula which takes its name from the Latin *in medio aquae* or 'in the midst of the waters'.

The vineyards of the Medoc, the most prestigious of the Bordelais, extend in a band some three to six miles wide and 50 miles long parallel with the left bank of the Gironde but separated from it by the *palus*, alluvial soil given over to pasture. Most of the vineyards are relatively recent, few having been planted before the 17th century – when the gently undulating landscape was a barren and isolated waste. Mostly Cabernet, Sauvignon, and Merlot, the vines are pruned low to get the heat reflected by the gravelly soil. Nearly all the wines marketed are reds – astringent, with great subtlety of flavour and an admirable bouquet. Due to their high iron content they have a tonic effect, though you do not need to be convalescing to justify drinking them.

Some 3,000 vineyards in the Bordelais produce wines of such excellence that they justify maturing in bottle. In 1855, at the World Fair in Paris, the best 62 of these were classified into five *crus* or growths. Of these 62, the wines of four châteaux – Lafite, Latour, Margaux, and Haut Brion – were judged on the basis of the prices they had commanded over the previous century to be supreme. They have held that position unchallenged until this day – except by one wine, that of Mouton Rothschild, classified in 1855 as the best of the second-growth clarets, a decision which raised a storm of controversy until its elevation to *premier cru* in 1973. It also created an intense rivalry between the brothers Philippe and Elie de Rothschild, owners of Mouton and Lafite, to such good effect that Mouton often commands higher prices than Lafite, labelled for years 'the world's most expensive wine'. Of these top five growths, four are in the Medoc.

North-east of Lamarque is Fort Medoc, built by Vauban (along with the citadel of Blaye on the opposite bank and Fort Pâté on an island in the river) to defend Bordeaux from the sea. The way north is on the winding D2 – passing close by many famous châteaux and giving vast scenic views of the Gironde.

Beyond Cussac is Château Beychevelle, a charmingly styled long and low building at the centre of 625 acres of vines, with its lawns going down to the river. Once owned by the irascible Duc d'Epernon, grand admiral of France in the 17th century, it is said to get its name from a corruption of *baisse-voile* or 'lower the sail', it being the custom for ships passing the Château to salute the Duke in this way.

There are no *grands crus* in the commune of St Julien but no one can accuse the municipality of being too modest. On entering the parish you are confronted by a notice saying *Passants, vous entrez ici dans le vignoble célèbre et séculaire de St Julien – Saluez!* The full *appellation* is in fact St Julien-Beychevelle. Here you are in the heartland of the Medoc, with great châteaux on either hand. West and north-west of St Julien are the châteaux of Lagrange and Talbot, the second taking its name from Shakespeare's 'old John Talbot', so renowned in France 'that no man in that kingdom dared encounter him in single combat'. The Château's Caillou Blanc is one of the few white Medocs produced. North of St Julien is Château Latour, producing a wine of hard masculine strength and great depth of flavour – with a full nose characteristic of the Cabernet-Sauvignon grape from which it is made. The Château, now partly British owned, has had a long and eventful history, the tower from which it takes its name having been built, they say, to give warning of the approach of Saracen pirates.

On a limestone hill to the north is Pauillac, wine capital of the Medoc though still only a small and sleepy town. It takes its name from the port beside the Gironde, the mellow old quays beside the river overlooked by its Maison du Vin. The vineyards hereabouts produce a richly flavoured wine with a bouquet of blackcurrants, a description which can be checked by tasting it at the *co-operative* on the outskirts.

Beyond Pauillac is Château Mouton Rothschild, a name well known in England. The 150 acres of vines surrounding the building are managed by

Baron Philippe, a man of wide ranging interests and talents (racing motorist, art collector, film producer, translator of English poetry). Since 1924 all the wine has been bottled at the Château. The Baron has built up a fascinating wine museum, the exhibits including tapestries, sculpture, and silverware. One of the most individual of the *premiers crus* Medocs, the richly flavoured wine has a suggestion of cedarwood in the bouquet.

North again, beside the D2 is what is generally regarded as the most important *grand cru classé* of the Bordelais: Château Lafite, owned by the Rothschild family since 1868 when the five brothers set out from the Frankfurt ghetto to make their fortunes. In the cellars are great vintages dating from 1797. The wine is a graceful combination of fruitiness and dryness with an underlying softness. The story goes that the Emir Abdul Kader, imprisoned at Amboise on the Loire, became seriously ill. His French doctor prescribed a diet that included Lafite. When he had tasted it, the Emir said that if only Mahomet had known the virtues of the divine beverage he might not have forbidden it in the Koran.

The village of St Estèphe, beside the Gironde to the north, is dominated by its church and occupies a hill islanded by vines – some 25,000 acres of them. Like Pauillac, St Estèphe has a river port and a *cave co-operative* offering tastings of its wines.

A short way on is St Seurin, at the northernmost limit of the Haut Medoc. Beyond it is the Bas Medoc, where most of the wines are made by *co-operatives* and covered by the generic *appellation* Medoc, though they are still very palatable. To continue the drive south through the Medoc the only feasible way is to return to Lamarque the way you came, on the D2.

West of Lamarque is Listrac, on a gravelly plateau well exposed to the sun. The earthy vigorous red wines produced by the local *co-operative* have a beautiful colour. Nearby Moulis is an ancient wine-producing centre with an interesting fortified church. Its red wines have great finesse, balance, and bouquet. Two notable named vineyards are Chasse Spleen and Grand Poujeaux. From Castelnau, on the main road south-west of Moulis, it is a straightforward drive through the vineyards to rejoin the D2. At Margaux, on higher ground astride the D2, the most notable vineyards are those backing the colonnaded façade of Château Margaux east of the village, a *premier cru classé* known the world over for its distinctive flavour and astonishing bouquet. You can visit the *cuverie* where the soft and scented wine is made, the *chais* where it is stored, and see the collection of old bottles it once went into. The main *chai*, over 300ft long, has an oak ceiling supported by huge stone pillars. Pavillon de Château Margaux is one of the little-known white wines of the Medoc. In the Château de Lascombes in the village is an exhibition of painting and sculpture devoted to wines and vines.

The ruined Château of Blanquefort near the D2 at the southern edge of the aristocratic Medoc holds the secret of the mysterious Dame Blanche, said to have been the daughter of a Moorish sultan who made his home here in the 8th century. On the way to Pessac on the western edge of Bordeaux one enters the Graves, named from its gravelly soil. Most of us think of Graves as a sweet white wine but it produces a fair number of reds as well, dry and with a characteristic *gout de terroir* or earthy taste. The generic *appellation* covers both kinds as well as a white Graves Supérieur of 12°. These are in fact the oldest vineyards in the Bordelais and in medieval England the red Graves were the best known and liked. They are richer tasting than the Medocs but less perfumed.

Near Pessac are the vineyards producing the remarkable red wines of Château Haut Brion, one of the five top growths in the Bordelais. The Château was owned for many years by the Pontac family, one member of which ran the *Royal Oak* tavern in Lombard Street in the City of London. A famous customer was Samuel Pepys, who wrote in his diary '. . . and here drank a sort of French wine called Ho Bryan that hath a good most particular taste that I never met with'. Across the road from Haut Brion is the Château de la Mission Haut Brion, recognisable by its enormous weathervane in the shape of a golden galleon. It dates from the 17th century and is named from the Congregation de la Mission or Lazaristes, the Order having been founded by St Vincent de Paul. The small vineyard on the brow of a hill on the left bank of the Garonne produces some of the most popular wines of the region. Marked in gold letters on the vaulted roof of the chapel in the Château are the best wine years of the last century.

East of Léognan, near by, are the vineyards of Château Carbonnieux, some of the most ancient in the Gironde, its wines being popular, so the story goes, when those of the Medoc were unknown. The Château was owned at one time by the Benedictine Abbey of Ste Croix du Mont, on the far side of the Garonne upstream, which exported its wines to all parts of the world. They say the monks sold their white wine to the court of the Turkish sultan, forbidden by his religion to drink wine, as 'mineral water of

Château de la brede – still the Montesquieu family home.

Carbonnieux'. The vines cover 430 acres – about a third are *cépages nobles* producing white wine, fragrant and subtly dry.

South-east of Léognan and still in the Graves is the lake-girt and harmoniously styled Château of Labrede, named from the *brede* or marsh that once surrounded it. The philosopher Montesquieu was born there in 1689 and the building, little changed, is still owned by his descendants. Here, he tended his vines and wrote his books and you can still see the study and library exactly as he left them. On the N113 to the east, in the small delimited district of Cérons, on the left bank of the Garonne, is Podensac, with the ruins of an 11th-century chapel and two 14th-century castles. The wine, of 12·5°, is a curious amalgamation of Graves and Premiers Côtes de Bordeaux from the other side of the river. On the same road, along the left bank of the Garonne, south of the town of Cérons, is Barsac – one of five communes in the Sauternais. Its soil is a mixture of gravel, clay, and limestone, its rows of Semillon and Sauvignon vines planted at right angles to the picturesque Céron valley. Six miles by four, the Sauternais is one of the smallest delimited areas in the Bordelais and consists of only five straggling villages: Barsac (the biggest), Sauternes, Fargues, Preignac, and Bommes. Containing a high degree of unfermented grape sugar, the magnificent sweet white wines of Sauternes and Barsac (so rich – or *liquoreux* as the French call it – that few people care for more than a glass or two at a time) are a delicate golden colour, with a powerful bouquet and a rarely matched intensity of flavour. The wines of 22 of the châteaux in the district, many of which welcome visitors for a tasting, were classified in 1855 into two growths, with Château Yquem in a class of its own. The designations Haut Barsac and Haut Sauternes, by the way, have only geographical significance.

What makes the Sauternais unique is the way the grapes are harvested, the bunches being left on the vines to develop the grey mould of *botrytis cinerea* and gathered one by one as they do so. The mould shrivels the grapes and evaporates much of their water content to leave a high concentration of sugar. The harvest starts around All Saints day and can go on for as long as two months, the *coupeurs* going over the same rows with long pointed scissors time and time again. If it rains, harvesting must stop and not restart until the sun has dried the grapes. If it rains for too long the ripest grapes fall to the ground or are desiccated by the mould. This way, growers can lose as much as two thirds of the crop. Pressings from the first grapes gathered make a wine called *vin de tête*, in good years *crème de tête*. The last grapes gathered produce *vin de queue* or tail.

What makes the operation particularly difficult is the climate. The Bordelais has an average 79 days rain between April and September and due to its nearness to the Atlantic a higher than average humidity in summer and autumn. The method of harvesting, the low yield (an acre of vines rarely produces more than 400 litres of must), and the fact that the wine is aged in the wood for a minimum of three years is what makes it expensive. A top growth Sauternes will literally go on improving in bottle for a lifetime. It is a wine to drink with strawberries and cream or as a mid-morning refresher.

Off the road linking Preignac and Sauternes are two notable châteaux. The first is the 17th-century Château de Malle, fronted by formal Italian gardens, with vineyards part in Graves, part in Sauternes. As well as the original furniture, the building has interesting architectural features. The second, a few miles south-west, is Château Yquem, incontestable king of white bordeaux, sharing its crown only with the Burgundian Montrachet. The vineyards cover 370 acres, of which 225 are planted with white grapes to make the famous Sauternes: in the ratio of three-quarters Semillon to one quarter Sauvignon, the first for elegance, the second for its astonishing bouquet. Local people say that anyone can make Sauternes of 15° alcohol – the difficulty is to make it half a degree higher, as Yquem usually is. But as the taste for sweet wines falls off, the Château is now making a drier Sauternes to be known as Château Ygrec (pronounced Ee-grek). But since the *appellation* laws require Sauternes to be sweet, it can only be called bordeaux blanc.

On the N113 south-east of Preignac, Langon is a prosperous little town and a market for the local wines which provided the setting for several of François Mauriac's novels. In the Brion valley a ten-minute drive to the south is the imposing feudal Château of Roquetaillade built in 1306 by a nephew of Pope Clement V, with six enormous round towers enclosing a rectangular *logis*. On a rocky platform above the opposite bank of the Garonne, and linked with Langon by a bridge across the river, picturesque St Macaire is a once-fortified small town dominated by the impressive St Sauveur Church and centred on the wide Marcadieu square bordered by *couverts* or covered walkways. The vineyards backing the town on the east, planted with the noble vines of Semillon, Sauvignon, and Muscadelle, are covered by the *appellation* Côtes de Bordeaux St Macaire.

From St Macaire a scenic road, the D10, follows the right bank of the Garonne as the river flows north-west to skirt the Premières Côtes de Bordeaux vineyards, the clayey soil producing red wines rich in tannin and sweet whites with a deep colour and a marked *gout de terroir* or earthy taste. At Ste-Croix-du-Mont, a village on a hill, there are pleasant wines for the tasting in the cellars of the *syndicat viticole* hewn out of the cliff by the river. There are also fine views from the terrace of the château near the church. Cadillac, a short way on, is a *bastide* founded in 1280 by Chaptal de Buch, companion-in-arms of the Black Prince. Behind the ruined ramparts facing the river is the moated Château Fayau, built by the Duke of Epernon in 1620, with cellars where one can sample the local red and white wines.

St Macaire is at the southern edge of the vast plateau covered by the fanciful *appellation* of Entre deux Mers, the two 'seas' in this context being the rivers Dordogne and Garonne bounding it on the north and south. Rich in old churches, pretty châteaux, and *caves co-operatives,* the rolling landscape provides sweeping views at nearly every turn. The wines, traditionally sweet, are now being vinified drier. To qualify for the Entre deux Mers *appellation* they must be made from at least 70 per cent Sauvignon, Semillon, and Muscadelle grapes.

A pretty road runs through the vineyards from St Macaire north-east to

Sauveterre de Guyenne, a typical English *bastide* founded in 1281, where there are four fortified gates and a vast central square bordered by arcades. It is named after its patron Abbey of La Sauve near Créon on the west, which itself takes its name from the forest (in Latin, *silva*) that covered the area until the monks cleared the land and planted the first vines in the 8th century.

The road north from Sauveterre to Castillon commands more attractive views as it passes close by the ruined Benedictine Abbey of Blasimon, the elegant façade of its 12th-century church enclosed by a fortified wall. The lively small town of Castillon was recently rechristened Castillon la Bataille to commemorate the French victory of 1453 that marked the end of Plantagenet rule in south-west France. Old John Talbot, champion of English arms and forty times a hero, was mortally wounded at the siege of Castillon, the prelude to the battle. Backing the town are the Côtes de Castillon vineyards, from which come generous reds of 11° and some delicate white wines. From Castillon, beside the Dordogne, the route turns west to follow the right bank of the river back to Blaye. The first important delimited area on the west is St Emilion, but the easiest and most pleasant way to reach it is to drive north from Castillon to St-Genes-de-Castillon, from there heading west through the vineyards on the scenic D17E.

Some 300 châteaux are contained within the *appellation* district surrounding the old hill and wine town of St Emilion. It embraces eight communes but five others (St Georges, Montagne, Lussac, Puisseguin, and Parsac) have the right to add it to their own name. The vineyards, in which the Roman system of irrigation is still used, are the oldest in the Gironde and produce the most full bodied of all red bordeaux, finely balanced and fruity. The district was marked out in a decree of 27 March 1289 by Edward I, King of England. The limestone clays covering the rocky subsoil are planted with the classic vine varieties of Cabernet, Malbec, Merlot, and Bouschet. One of the most important châteaux is Ausone, named after the 4th-century Latin poet of Bordelais origin, its cellars adapted from ancient grottoes.

The curious up-and-down settlement of St Emilion, in a charming situation on two horseshoe-shaped hills facing south, is named after the saint who sought refuge there from the Saracens in the 8th century. The subterranean church at the junction of the two hills, with its nave and two aisles carved out of one block of stone, is one of the oldest in France. Flanking the church are caves and catacombs. In the town is a wine museum and the 12th-century tasting cellars of the Manoir du Pont Levis.

At Montagne north of St Emilion is the Château des Tours, built in the 13th century and restored in the 16th century by Viollet le Duc. Covered by the *appellation* Montagne-St-Emilion, the 200 acres of vines surrounding the Château, one of the most impressive in the district, produce a red wine little different from a St Emilion.

From Montagne a byway leading to Libourne on the west passes through the Pomerol vineyards, first planted by the Knights Templars in the 12th century. They produce a delectable red wine with a multiplicity of flavour and aroma. A long list of châteaux – Beauregard, Sales, Conseillante, La Croix de Gay, Nenin, and Certain – welcome visitors, asking only for a *coup de téléphone* beforehand. Dating from 1270, the *bastide* of Libourne astride the Dordogne takes the name of its founder Sir Roger de Leybourne, *sénéschal de Guyenne* or representative in Aquitaine of the English king. In the thriving port, from which the local wines go out to all parts of the world, English ships tied up in the Middle Ages. Libourne stands at the southern edge of the Pomerol district and the northern edge of another called Graves de Vayres, bisected by the old Roman road linking Paris and Bordeaux, and producing good white wines and even better reds.

Reaching down to the right bank of the Dordogne on the west of Libourne is the delimited area of Fronsac, from which comes firmly styled and robust red wines with a fruity bouquet. Beside the river, the ancient town of Fronsac is overlooked by the Tertre plateau on which once stood a fortress built by Charlemagne. North of St-Michel-de-Fronsac, a short way downstream, is the beautiful Château-de-la-Rivière, isolated amid its vines. Below the Château are extensive cellars hewn out of the rock which, with their rich store of wine, were concealed from the Germans occupying the building during the war by placing flowers at the only entrance to make it look like a tomb.

Beyond the important road junction of St-André-de-Cubzac, the road along the right bank of the river becomes a *corniche* giving fine views of the valleys of the Dordogne and, later, the Gironde. Soon after Prignac, on the way to Bourg, the road passes near the prehistoric grottoes of Pair-non-Pair and, in season, a tasting stand manned by the *cave co-operative* based at nearby Tauriac. Bourg, on the right bank of the Dordogne, looks across to the river's junction with the Garonne, separated by an alluvial *bec* or beak now occupied by refineries. On a limestone hill, the sleepy old town consists of two parts, a once-fortified upper quarter and another at river level built around its port, with steep streets and steps linking the two. The vine-cloaked slopes behind the town produce a lot of wine, the best of which are whites covered by the Côtes de Bourg *appellation*. North-east of Bourg is the village of Lansac, with the 11th-century monastery of La Croix Davide which a thousand years ago provided food and shelter for pilgrims on the way to Santiago de Compostella in northern Spain.

The pretty corniche road continues along the riverside to Blaye, on the right bank of the Gironde, starting point and terminus of this route through the Bordelais. The aristocratic *crus* of the Bordelais are important, of course, but the real strength of the region is the enormous range in quality and style of its non-vintage wines from *petits châteaux, co-operatives,* and little-known growers. Seeking these out is interesting enough, but an added bonus are the reminders round almost every corner of one of the most fascinating periods in English history.

# Cognac

Contained within the two *départements* of Charente between the Limousin and the coast north of Bordeaux, the area where cognac is made is carefully marked out into concentric wine-growing districts not unlike an archery target – and the nearer one gets to the bullseye the better it is. Whilst knowing where one district ends and another begins certainly helps one's appreciation of this aristocrat of brandies, it is not at all essential to the enjoyment of the area itself. Little explored, despite the enormous prestige of the spirit it sends to every corner of the globe, the Cognac region also contributes many unexportable attractions. The list includes the meandering Charente – 'the fairest river in my kingdom', according to Henri IV – along with other bucolic rivers and streams, lush water-meadows that provide the finest butter in France, hundreds of graceful Romanesque churches with sculptured façades and massive yet elegant choirs, lichen-hung castle ruins dating from the Hundred Years' War, sleepy villages of golden stone dispersed in a green landscape, and vineyards that roll away over brightly lit hills and dales.

Happily this is a part of France not geared to tourism, so that modest inns are more plentiful than luxury hotels, and *bistrots* that scorn a menu are easier to find than restaurants with plate-glass frontages. The atmosphere is tranquil and relaxed. The Charentais are called by their neighbours *cagouilles* after the big snails that feed in their vineyards, which is another way of saying they refuse to be hurried.

But the charm of this sunny and beautifully lethargic region with its mellow maritime climate is in its countryside, beside the poplar-lined rivers and in the peaceful villages – in sum, in its genuine rusticity. 'Claret is the liquor for boys, port for men, but he who aspires to be a hero must drink brandy', said Samuel Johnson. He might have gone on to explain that while brandy may not be cognac, all cognac is brandy. Brandy can be made wherever grapes will ripen, simply by double distilling the fermented juice. But cognac is something else again.

Cognac can only be made from grapes grown and fermented into white wine within one of six delimited areas called *crus*. Working outwards from the heartland, the best district, in descending order of quality, these are: Grande Champagne, Petite Champagne, Borderies, Fins Bois, Bons Bois, and Bois Ordinaires. Vine varieties growing in these open chalklands are strictly controlled, too, being mainly confined to the St Emilion, Folle Blanche (the Picpoul of Armagnac), and Colombard. Except that Grande Champagne and the better-known Champagne around Reims are both on chalky soils, hence the name, there is no connection between the two.

History and not providence decided that the mediocre wine of the region – thin, acid, and earthy, rarely attaining 10° of alcohol and more often only 7° – should turn into brandy. Not that the strength of the wine matters much. Within reason, the lower its alcohol content the better the spirit distilled from it. Distilling is a winter activity, starting as soon as the wine has fermented in November and going on until April. It is carried out mostly by individual growers – some 6,000 of them – using their own pot stills in their big isolated farmhouses, originally designed for security against marauders and completely enclosing an inner courtyard. Made of copper, the stills have changed little since the Middle Ages, though the process and the end-result are strictly controlled.

The first distillation consists simply of heating up the wine to 85°C and condensing the vapour. Since alcohol boils at a lower temperature than water the alcohol vapours come off first and are condensed back into liquid form as they pass through coiled pipes cooled in various ways, most often by passing them through the wine waiting to be heated. The result is a milky white liquid with a neutral taste some 30° strong called *brouillis*. The beginning (the 'head') and end (the 'tail') of the distilled liquid is discarded, and the 'heart' is distilled again.

Known as the *bonne chauffe*, the second distillation is critical: the heat is carefully controlled to regulate the temperature of the liquid so as to guarantee its final purity. Once the process has started it cannot be stopped and during the whole of this time the still must be watched day and night.

As it comes out of the still the finished spirit is as clear as water. Once again the head and tail are cut off, only the heart being kept for maturing and eventual drinking. Even at this stage the brandy is harsh and, with an alcohol strength of about 70°, too strong. It is in this state that many growers sell the distilled spirit to the great brandy shippers in Cognac, Jarnac, and elsewhere, the chief taster of each deciding what he will buy for blending with his grown-up cognacs. But first the spirit must be matured, in casks of oak from the Limousin or, since wood from this source is becoming scarce, from the great oak forest of Tronçais near Bourges.

The staves from which the barrels are made are aged for five years in the open before being sent to the cooper, who shapes them and rings them together with hoops of iron. He then places the skeleton barrel over a fire while wetting it on the outside. This bends the staves and shapes the barrel at the same time as it makes it spirit-tight.

No cognac may be sold until it has aged in cask for three years, during which time some of the strength – as much as 30° – and all the harshness will have faded away. So also will a percentage of the cognac, a loss which is known as 'the angels' share'. Blending came about partly because every cask has to be topped up to replace this loss of about 3 per cent a year. As it ages, the spirit takes colour from the tannin in the oak and develops its bouquet and taste. But only part of the colour comes from the wood: caramel is legitimately allowed to help. The long low *chais* or warehouses where the casks are stored are easily recognizable. Over the years a unique fungus, nurtured by the fumes, turns the exteriors of their roofs black.

After being matured and blended with others of different years and different districts some cognacs are further aged in cask. A few vintage cognacs are of one good year only, a *millesimé*, put to one side by individual growers for a rainy day and when it rained selling them to the shippers. Along with venerable cognacs they have aged themselves, the shippers store them in an inner sanctum called the *paradis* – though if they are more than 50 years old they are likely to be kept in glass rather than wood. Some shippers have reserves of up to 50 million bottles, worth a fortune even in Greek shipowner terms. A Napoléon brandy is one drawn from a cask started in the Emperor's day, of which some has evaporated and some has been drawn off – the loss having been made good with a younger cognac. The spirit ages only in cask, not in bottle, and the Napoléon concerned is almost bound to be the third of the line, not the first. Vintage liqueur cognac is a term no longer permitted by French law. The letters VSOP on the label stand for Very Superior Old Pale, not *verser sans oublier personne* as some humorists will tell the unsuspecting. Cognac labelled *fine champagne* comes exclusively from grapes grown in the two best districts of Grande and Petite Champagne.

A good cognac should be dry and smooth, with a clean chestnut colour and a bouquet reminiscent of the vine in flower. Before tasting it, the drinker should warm the balloon glass it is served in with the palm of his hand and slowly inhale the aroma.

A highly original apéritif made in the region since the 16th century from a matured blend of unfermented grape juice and cognac is Pineau de Charentes, sweet and strong and with its own *appellation contrôlée*. It began as a way to make newly distilled cognac drinkable; there are about 60 places in the region where it can be tasted. The juice comes from the Pineau grape, which gives the drink its name.

The port of La Rochelle in the Bois Ordinaires district 20 miles north-west of the Charente estuary was engaged in exporting wine long before Bordeaux. Its maritime trade began soon after the collapse of the Roman empire, when ships from England and other countries to the north arrived to take on what in those days was one of the most precious of minerals, salt, made by evaporating seawater along the coast of western France. By 1190 La Rochelle was known throughout the western world and possessed not one but two ports, one created on the orders of the Plantagenet Henry II, Duke of Guyenne and Count of Poitiers. Exports of salt soon took second place to wines from the Poitou vineyards that covered much of the area between the Loire and the Gironde. In 1197 the Abbot of Mont St Michel on the coast of Normandy recorded the sinking in a terrible storm of over 30 ships, all laden with wines from La Rochelle. Most wines from these vineyards were white, which continued to be in great demand for centuries. But in the early 17th century they were judged small and thin by English shippers and by 1750 the vineyards were in decline. Dutch merchants had been among the biggest buyers of Poitou wines. Indeed, they had dominated the wine trade in western France for generations, and it was due to their initiative that the vineyards had been replanted and extended. Again under their influence came the distillation of wine into *eaux de vie* or water of life. Until then it had been made in secret by alchemists and was thought of only as a medicine. Once it became a peasant activity, the wood used for heating the stills soon deforested the region. *Eaux de vie* then took the name given it by the Dutch merchants who imported it just as eagerly as they had imported the wines. The name was *brandewijn* or burnt wine, our version of this becoming brandy.

Paradoxically, one of the last parts of the region to turn from making wine to distilling spirit was the Charente basin centred on Cognac – famed in the Middle Ages for producing some of the best wines of the region – as it now produces the best cognac. The first record of the change was in 1725, when the distillation was still being referred to as *eaux de vie de Cognac*. The wine made into cognac may be mediocre, but drinkable *vins de pays* are still produced in the region – like the dry golden wines of Châteauneuf-sur-Charente or the agreeable reds of Jonzac, Barbezieux, and Ségonzac. They are interesting wines to drink where they are made and worth asking for in local restaurants.

Cognac has one of the richest cuisines in France, most dishes being cooked in butter and many being flavoured with cognac or Pineau. The coast being under half an hour's drive to the west, seafood is both plentiful and fresh. Cultivated at many places near the sea, oysters are often served in the shell with tiny garlic-flavoured sausages or *à la charentaise* with pâté. *Mouclade* is a soup made of mussels but also contains cream, yolk of egg, white wine, and butter. A *chaudrée*, on the other hand, is a soup made of freshwater fish. From the rivers, too, come little *goujons* or gudgeons fried in batter as a *friture*. Sole often comes stuffed with goose liver, lobsters are excellent, and the *crevettes* or shrimps are among the best in France. The savoury pâtés include some made from *grive* or thrush and *caille* or quail, and there are tasty *andouillettes* and *boudin* sausages, and tender cuts from maize-fed pork. Mushroom and truffle omelettes *au cognac*, *cagouilles* or snails fed on vine leaves, and soufflé-like *mousselines* of salmon, pike, and trout all form part of many menus. A number of dishes are based on *confits* or preserved meat of goose, duck, and pork. Equally satisfying are the turkeys flavoured with Pineau. Ham, grilled or braised and served with grapes, is popular, as is tripe flavoured with garlic and steaks grilled over *sarments* or vine shoots. The famed *jambonneau de poularde* of Barbezieux is a succulent boned and stuffed leg of chicken, though in this as in other towns chicken and capon are prepared in numerous ways.

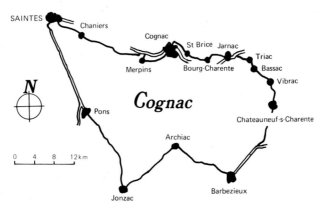

On its way to the Atlantic, the river Charente runs east-west across the region, marking the northern border of Grande Champagne as it flows past the brandy-filled warehouses of the old town of Cognac, the main centre. But cognac is also made and marketed along the river at Saintes in the Fins Bois on the west and at Jarnac, on the borders of Grande Champagne and Fins Bois on the east. Other centres are Ségonzac, in the Grande Champagne south-east of Cognac, and, in Petite Champagne on the east, south-east, and south, Châteauneuf, Barbezieux, Jonzac, and Archiac. The suggested tour that follows takes in most of these places and being circular can be started and finished at any point along the way. The yellow Michelin maps 71 and 72 cover the region.

The ancient grey town of Cognac is centred on the château, unimpressive on the outside, fascinating within, where the French King François I was born in 1494. The castle was built by Jean de Valois on return from his long captivity in England at the close of the Hundred Years' War. The pretty town hall is in an unusually attractive and peaceful setting: a public park. Apart from the 12th-century Romanesque St Lager Church, the main attractions are the riverside *chais* of the cognac shippers, their roofs blackened by the fungus that lives off the fumes rising up from the maturing brandy. One can go to any or all of them for a tour of the cellars and a tasting. More dramatically interesting, perhaps, is a visit to the St Gobain glassworks on the outskirts, where, wholly by automation, bottles of all shapes and colours are made for the brandy shippers.

A minor road follows the north bank of the river upstream to St Brice, with a 16th-century château in a fine park and remarkable statues in the 12th-century church. Along the river to the east is the peaceful village of Bourg Charente, where the waters divide into several branches. The church is pretty and the château dominating the village dates from the time of Henry IV. To the south, on the far side of the river, a scenic road leads to the quaint old village of Ségonzac.

Still on the north bank of the river, the road goes on to Jarnac, which over the last couple of centuries has added to its role as an agricultural market another as a centre for cognac. In this sense it is almost as important as Cognac itself, and there are several cellars at which to call for a tasting. On 10 July 1547 a duel was fought at Jarnac between Chabot, the local seigneur, and Chataigneraie, a favourite of Henri II, in front of the King, the Queen, and the King's mistress Diane de Poitiers. On the point of being beaten, Chabot unexpectedly delivered a fatal thrust to his opponent, an act which in France has unjustly passed into history as the *coup de Jarnac* or treacherous blow.

Beside the road between the villages of Triac and Bassac is a pyramid-shaped monument commemorating the victory in 1569 of the Catholics over the Protestants during the religious wars, a battle in which the Prince of Condé was slain. Blood ran high and flowed freely during this period, for the region was and still is predominantly Protestant. The beautiful church at Bassac forms part of a great abbey founded in 1002 which was sacked during the Hundred Years' War and deserted by the Benedictines in 1666. It has since been re-occupied by a missionary order. There are fine views of the Charente valley from the village.

To the south-east, in a wide loop of the river, is the delightful small town of Châteauneuf. The Romanesque church above the town has an abundantly sculptured façade in the Saintonge style characteristic of the region. Pleasant gardens line the river.

The capital of Petite Champagne, the cheerful old town of Barbezieux to the south-east, is bisected by the busy *route nationale* 10. Built on the slope of a hill, its maze of narrow streets is dominated by a 15th-century château. The town specializes in making goose-liver pâté and fruits preserved in cognac, and the local restaurants create a variety of dishes from the fine chickens and capons reared in the district.

Over to the west, the vineyards around the small town of Archiac are highly thought of. Nearby Jonzac is an agreeable provincial town hosting the premises of several cognac *négociants* as well as a *co-operative* where you can taste the brandy and the Pineau. The heart of the town is the beautifully preserved and multi-towered 15th-century château, from the terrace of which there are fine views of the Seugne valley.

The main N137 passing north-south through the charming small town of Pons, north-west of Jonzac, was the route taken in the Middle Ages by pilgrims on the way to Santiago de Compostella in northern Spain. Pons is built on a hill beside the river Sauldre which reflects in its waters the 12th-century castle, keep, and ramparts that were the one-time home of a noble family who ruled 600 parishes all around – and who were answerable only to the king. The pilgrims' hospice built outside the ramparts, so that travellers could find shelter even at night when the town gates were closed, is one of the few to have survived. One can visit the dormitory and the hospital where pilgrims taken ill were cared for and see the ruined chapel where they prayed. On the walls of a vaulted passage that linked the hospice with the chapel are graffiti carved by the pilgrims while they waited for a storm or the heat of mid-day to pass.

To reach the hospice at Pons (pronounced pon) the pilgrims crossed the river Charente at Saintes, on the north-west, a spacious shady town rich in ancient monuments. There are many old houses in the web of narrow streets in the old quarter bordering the Charente south of the Cours Nationale – the main street running east-west through the town. Two important relics of Roman times are the triumphal arch dedicated to Tiberius near the bridge across the river and on the south-western outskirts the amphitheatre set in a ravine topped by the pilgrimage Church of St Eutrope, with its crypt housing the tomb of the Saint.

The return to Cognac on the east is best made on the pretty road running mostly along the north bank of the Charente. It passes through the village of Cheniers, with its part-fortified Romanesque church, and, soon after the highway crosses the river, the remains of the Roman station of Condate at Merpins – also notable for its ruined Cistercian abbey, Celtic oppidum, and feudal château, moats, and ramparts. In the early stages, particularly, the road gives pleasant views of the water meadows that line the river.

# Loire valley

For its food and wine as much as for its châteaux reflected in limpid waters, the most attractive part of the Loire valley lies in the extensive old provinces of Touraine and Anjou. Set in a peaceful green landscape of low wooded hills and bathed in a softly luminous atmosphere, the smiling and spacious river is bordered by bathing beaches and ancient slate-roofed villages and small towns backed by limestone cliffs honeycombed with cellars where the wines mature. Most of the châteaux are in Touraine but downstream, too, the river flows past old castles and manor houses, reminders of the days when the English Plantagenet kings were also lords of Anjou.

The wines of both provinces were well liked in 12th-century England, though later they lost ground to those of Bordeaux. Then, Flemish merchants based at Nantes, near the mouth of the Loire, sailed their ships upstream as far as Saumur to take on the top quality *vins de mer*, leaving the lesser *vins de terre* to be sent overland to Paris.

Nowadays, the absence of any kind of river traffic enhances the charm of the meandering river. From its unpolluted waters comes a variety of fish, some of which – such as pike and *alose* or shad – end up on the tables of the riverside restaurants accompanied by the famous *beurre blanc*, a subtle blend of white wine, shallots, vinegar and butter. There may perhaps be nothing spectacular about other items on the bill of fare, but being cooked in traditional ways and based on succulent ingredients from this 'garden of France', they are easily recognizable and appeal both to the eye and the palate. The gastronome Curnonsky, born at Angers, the old capital of Anjou, unwittingly described the cuisine of the valley when he said that food was good when things tasted of what they were.

Restaurant meals in Touraine invariably begin with savoury *rillettes* or potted pork, those in Anjou often end with tiny *cremets* or cream cheeses dusted with sugar. In between might come *palourdes farcies* (stuffed clams), a mixed fish fry called *friture de la Loire*, a wine-dark *matelote* of eel, *noisettes de porc aux pruneaux* (loin of pork with prunes), or in season richly flavoured game from the forests.

The wines grown along these reaches of the Loire are as varied and as charming as the landscape. In Touraine, the vineyards come into view more often along its tributaries than they do beside the Loire itself, most of those in the valley being planted on the far side of the limestone bluffs rising up from the river. Here as in Anjou most of these hills are tunnelled into by long cool cellars where the wines sleep at a constant temperature waiting for the moment when their corks are pulled and their fragrance is released. Happily many of these cellars, in which conditions are perfect for tasting the wines, are open to visitors.

Probably the finest and best-known wine of Touraine is the amber coloured and delicately perfumed Vouvray, but there are reds and rosés as well. Vouvray comes from the Chenin Blanc or Pineau de la Loire, the variety of vine most successful on the chalky clay covering the coarse limestone of the upper slopes. Cabernet Franc, Gamay, Pinot Noir, and Pinot Gris cloak the low-lying gravel around Chinon and elsewhere. Some vineyards in Touraine are planted with Sauvignon, one of the great white wine grapes of France, and were given an *appellation* as recently as 1969. Most of the white wines either take the generic name of Touraine, one of the districts within it such as Bourgeuil, or a combination of the two like Touraine-Amboise.

The fresh and lively wines of Anjou – 18 of them covered by an *appellation contrôlée* – are the most interesting and satisfying of all those grown along the Loire. Over half of them are white, the balance being made up of rosés and a few reds which are difficult to find even in local restaurants.

Some of the whites are made into *petillant* or semi-sparkling wine, particularly around Saumur in the eastern part of the province, but the best are the still wines. As in Touraine, the finest white wines come from the Chenin Blanc, grown in Anjou since the 9th century. The reds are made from Cabernet, the rosés from Groslot, Gamay, and other varieties (though as their name implies, the fruity, clean-tasting, and often strong Rosés de Cabernet are made only from two varieties of Cabernet grapes). The hills around Saumur are of limestone but downstream near Angers the thin layer of topsoil covers hard rock which the growers often have to break up before they can plant their vines.

Districts with their own *appellation* are the Coteaux de la Loire, on both sides of the river east and west of Angers; the Coteaux du Layon, on the flanks of the long stream of that name flowing north-west to enter the Loire in western Anjou, producing the unctuous and fruity white wines high in alcohol which in good years are made from grapes gathered after they have been attacked by *pourriture noble* or noble rot; the small Coteaux de l'Aubance, near the left bank of the Loire south of Angers, with its white and rosé wines little known outside the region; and, over to the east, along the left bank of the Loire upstream from Saumur, the Coteaux de Saumur, the dry and lively white, rosé, and red wines of which are grown behind the cliffs hollowed out with deep cellars and riverside cave dwellings.

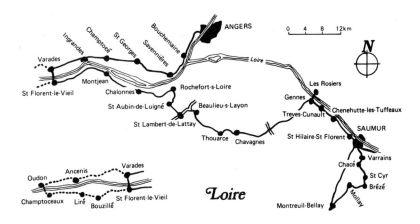

Most roads through the vineyards along this part of the Loire are little-frequented and scenic *routes départementales*. The main N152 along the right bank of the river between Tours and Angers is a popular through-route, though it offers some fine views. But the *départementales* or the equally well surfaced *voies ordinaires* are the ones with the quietest hotels and camping sites, of which there is almost always a choice. Road bridges cross the Loire at many points, though occasionally the lack of one involves a longish detour. The yellow Michelin maps 63 and 64 cover the region.

Some of the easternmost vineyards of Touraine are those around Amboise, originally planted not by the monks like many others in the province but by order of the local lord. Rising up above the mellow old town on the left bank of the Loire, here divided by a central island spanned by the bridge linking it with either bank, is the massive castle from which the young King François II, along with Catherine de Médici and the rest of his court, coolly watched the slaughter of the 1,500 Huguenots who had planned to kidnap him. As it happened, the imbecilic François was the last French monarch ever to occupy the building. Near the castle is the 15th-century manor of Clos Lucé, the home of Leonardo da Vinci for the few years leading up to his death.

In the cemetery adjoining the Church of St Denys, in the town, is the grave of the Duc de Choiseul, able and patriotic minister of Louis XV, to whom the King gave the castle of Amboise in 1762. But the Duke did not enjoy it for long. A few years later he was banished for refusing to acknowledge the authority of the King's mistress Madame Dubarry. Still standing beside the D31 to Bléré, a few miles south, is the Pagode de Chanteloup – a folly he built to commemorate those who visited him in his exile.

From the village of Nazelles north-west of Amboise the scenic byway D1 runs west along the Cisse stream parallel with the Loire to Noizay, the wines of which come within the Vouvray *appellation*. The Chenin Blanc vines from which the wine is made are pruned abnormally low to minimise the risk of frost damage. Since 1880 a fair proportion of the wine has been made

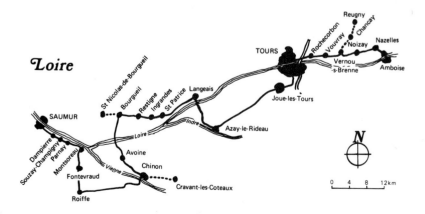

*mousseux* or sparkling. From the prosperous little town of Vernou-sous-Brenne it is a pleasant drive north along the river through Chancey to Reugny, one of the best-known Vouvray growths. Equally enjoyable is the short run west from Vernou to the charming small town of Vouvray, at the point where the Cisse flows into the Loire, famed for its wine since the 15th century. The best place to sample the vintage is in one of the cool dark cellars hewn out of the cliffs, such as Bassereau or Boucq, or the Cave de la Vallée Coquette, its fine Vouvrays coming from the pretty little valley of that name west off the riverside road to Tours. Visible from afar, and possibly familiar even to those who have never seen it before, is the square and slender 14th-century watchtower reproduced on the labels of the delicate wine made at the elongated village of Rochecorbon. One of the best growths is Clos Martin, and one of the best-known wines the sparkling Blanc Foussy – waiting to be sampled at the Caves St Roch. More impressive, though, are the nearby cellars of Marc Bredif.

A few miles west in the angle formed by the junction of the A10 motorway and the N152 along the right bank of the Loire is the Abbey of Marmoutier, founded in the 4th century by St Martin, the Roman soldier who shared his cloak with a beggar. When Pope Urban II preached the first Crusade there in 1095 the Abbey was already one of the richest and most powerful in France. All that remains now is the gate used only by the mitred abbot, a combined belfry and keep, and the burial chambers and sanctuaries hollowed out of the steep cliff bordering the grounds on the south. The most important of these is the Chapel of the Seven Sleepers and the nearby grotto containing their tombs. The story goes that the Seven, all disciples of the Saint and all related to each other, died a natural death simultaneously exactly 25 years after St Martin himself and that their corpses subsequently brought about numerous miracles.

Another legend has it that the monks learned by accident of the virtue of pruning vines. While everyone was at prayer some donkeys broke loose in the extensive Abbey vineyards and ate all the vine shoots. The monks thought their vineyards were finished but to their astonishment the following year the vines grew stronger than before and the grapes they bore were the finest they had ever seen. The vineyards of Vouvray and Rochecorbon owe their origin entirely to the painstaking husbandry of the monks of Marmoutier.

Any motorist driving on a north-south line through Tours could be forgiven for writing it off as just another spaghetti junction. The damage done to the town in 1940, its rapid growth since the war, and its position at the crossing of important road routes have all helped to give it a modern look – yet this is one of the most historic places in the Loire valley. Here, St Martin, the apostle of the Gauls, was bishop; here, Gregory of Tours, the first French historian, recorded the passing scene; and here, Alcuin of York founded the first school of theology in France. At least the finest churches have been spared and the main street, the Rue Nationale, has been reconstructed much as it used to be. In the Rue Nationale are the Celliers St Julien, with a wide range of Touraine wines for the tasting. A mile or two south of Tours is Joué-les-Tours, famed for its red wine.

Bisecting Joué is the N751 leading south-west to Azay-le-Rideau on the right bank of the wooded Indre. Islanded in the river is the most beautiful Renaissance château of the Loire. The local wine bears the *appellation* Touraine-Azay-le-Rideau. From Azay a minor road runs north-west along the Indre before branching off to pass through Lignières and cross the Loire to Langeais. Occupying a promontory in the centre of the town, the small fortress is one of the most interesting in the region. Not only does it remain exactly as it was when built in the 15th century, it has also kept its original furnishings. South-west of Langeais, off the main road along this side of the Loire, is St Patrice, starting point of the drive west through the Bourgeuil vineyards. St Nicolas de Bourgeuil is said to make better wine than its big brother Bourgeuil a short way east, the centre for the wines grown in the villages of Benais, Ingrandes, Restigné, and others round about. One notable sight in Bourgeuil is the spacious Angevin choir in the Church of St Germain, another the cellars of the Divine Bottle (Dive Bouteille) incorporating a small wine museum, where one vintage to try if available might be the elegant and rarely tracked down Bourgeuil rosé.

The 'red velvet' wines of Bourgeuil are said to give off a perfume of raspberries, those of nearby Chinon one of violets, but otherwise there is little difference between them. Both come from the small black grape of the Cabernet Franc, the variety so widely planted in the Medoc. At both places the vine, called Breton locally, is pruned with a *taille longue*: one long lateral shoot of ripened wood that bears the grapes.

From Bourgeuil the road to Chinon on the Vienne crosses the Loire near the Centrale Nucleaire powerhouse and cuts across the Veron, an isolated and often-flooded tongue of land separating the two rivers. Strung out on a ledge between the right bank of the river and the wooded hills behind, the old town of Chinon reminds the visitor, at almost every step, of its famous son Rabelais and the vermilion-coloured and full-flavoured wine he loved so well. Towering above is the majestic ruined castle, or rather three castles in one, where Henry II of England died in 1189 and where in 1429 Joan of Arc singled out the French King Charles VII from among his courtiers.

Most of the Chinon *appellation* vineyards are around Cravant-les-Coteaux to the east, though one of the best growths is the famous Clos de l'Echo near the town itself, which some say Rabelais once owned. The wine can be tasted at the Cave du Syndicat in the town; an unusual variation that may be on offer there is Chinon Blanc.

Off the Loudun road on the far side of the Vienne, the byway to Roiffé passes close by La Devinière, the cottage pompously dubbed manor where Rabelais is supposed to have been born. North of Roiffé and across the border in Anjou is the big village of Fontevraud, which makes some wine but is better known for its great abbey (used until a few years ago as a prison). Protected by the dukes of Anjou, this was once one of the wealthiest religious foundations in France. In the church, the 'Westminster of the Plantagenets', are the tombs of Henry II, his wife Eleanor of Aquitaine, his son Richard the Lionheart, and his daughter-in-law Isabel of Angoulême.

The main road going north from Fontevraud joins the Loire again at

Montsoreau, rising in terraces above the river, whose wine has a character all its own. From the pretty château, once washed by the river, there are fine views of the wide expanse of water formed by the junction of the Loire and the Vienne. The pleasant drive west to Saumur along this, the left bank of the Loire, is the *route du vin* of the Coteaux de Saumur, the wines of which owe their distinctive flavour to the chalk subsoil hereabouts. The road runs between the gently shelving river bank and a line of hills breaking out here and there into white cliffs. The *coteaux* starts at Montsoreau and ends at Dampierre, though the better-known names are in between: Parnay, and, celebrated for its remarkable red wine, Souzay-Champigny. At Souzay is the manor where Marguerite of Anjou lived, wife of the English King Henry VI. Two tasting cellars to bear in mind are the Cave sous Roc at Parnay and the Caveau du Vieux Pressoir at Dampierre.

Saumur is said to take its name from a monastery ringed by ramparts (*salvus muris* in Latin) that was founded in the 10th century by Thibault, Lord of Touraine. The town sprawls over both banks of the Loire and an island in between – all linked by a multi-arched bridge.

In a superb setting beside the river is the imposing 14th-century château depicted in its original splendour as a backdrop to a vineyard scene in the famous miniature of the *Très Riches Heures du Duc de Berry* now in the Condé museum at Chantilly. Saumur is famed for its Cadre Noir cavalry school and in the château is a museum devoted to the horse. Adjoining the viticultural school on the south-western outskirts of the town is the 12th-century Church of Notre Dame de Nantilly housing the richest collection of tapestries in the whole of France.

The restaurants of Saumur are noted for the way they prepare two of the most prized fish of the Loire, pike and shad. Two local specialities are *pâté de sarcelle* or teal pie, a bird regarded with 'tongue-in-cheek' on fast days as a fish, and *pâté de lamproie*, the cross between an eel and a fish that we call lamprey. Vast quantities of mushrooms are grown in the cellars cut out of the riverside bluffs on either side of the town.

South of Saumur, beyond the 60ft-long megalithic monument called le Grand Dolmen beside the N138, are the vine-cloaked valleys of the Thouet and the canalised Dive, two of the many tributaries of the Loire. Last in a string of wine villages (Varrains, Chacé, St-Cyr-en-Bourg) is Brézé, with a castle once owned by the Maillé family – one member of which in 1548 escorted Mary Queen of Scots to France to marry the Dauphin. Varrains is at the centre of the red wine Cabernet vineyards of Saumur-Champigny and of the Coteaux de Saumur. Demanding to be seen are the enormous cellars at the Cave Co-operative des Vignerons at St-Cyr-en-Bourg.

From Brézé, a restful road follows the Thouet to the charming village of Montreuil Bellay. It is dominated by its 15th-century castle, a genuine fortress built for defence and still ringed by a great wall. Viewed from the inner courtyard, the turrets, dormers, and towers are a fantastic sight. The village is noted for its goats' cheese and for the rosé wines made by the Compagnie de la Vallée de la Loire. On the N138 is the tasting cellar with the seemingly contradictory name of the Caveau du Presbytère. On the scenic highway along the left bank of the Loire north-west of Saumur are the twin villages of St-Hilaire-St-Florent, where one of the 16 sparkling wines in France with an *appellation contrôlée* is made in great quantities by both the *methode champenoise* and the *cuve close*. St Florent has a 13th-century church in Angevin Gothic and vast *caves* hollowed out of the hillside where the secondary fermentation in bottle takes place. In addition to a dry white wine there is or should be a sweet rosé for the tasting. As well as the cellars, a unique stone museum and another devoted to mushroom cultivation are worth a visit.

Nearby Chenehutte-les-Tuffeaux takes its name from its pale-grey cliffs of *tuffeaux* or micaceous chalk, typical of the stone worked by generations of church, château, and house builders in Anjou. Beyond the feudal keep of Treves is the splendid Romanesque Church of Cunault, the only surviving part of a Benedictine priory suppressed on the eve of the French Revolution. The ornately sculptured capitals of the columns are just one feature of the majestic interior.

Backed by wooded heights and on a hill giving fine views of the valley, Gennes also has white cliffs cut into by troglodyte dwellings that, cool in summer and warm in winter, are still occupied. Some have façades of masonry or brick flush with the hillside, and chimneys poking up out of the fields above. As the French writer Théophile Gautier said, people living in them have little else to do but wait for the rabbits to fall into their cooking pots. Or, he might have added, the fish to swim into their nets anchored in the Loire. The restaurateurs of Gennes excel at making *brochet au beurre blanc* from the young pike caught in the river.

The wines of Gennes come under the *appellation* Coteaux de l'Aubance, like those of the charming village of Les Rosiers on the far side of the suspension bridge across the Loire, with its old houses and 13th-century church. The road that cuts south-west through the forest from Gennes to Thouarce enters the Coteaux du Layon vineyards at Chavagnes, where a wine festival is held during the grape harvest on the second Sunday in October. Beside the N784 through the village is the Caveau du Petit Val. Thouarce, dominated by its Romanesque belfry above the Layon, is a centre for some of the choicest wines in all France. On the left bank of the stream and with its own *appellation* is Bonnezeaux, its vineyards topped by an ancient windmill. The full ripe wine can be tasted at the Bonnezeaux-Relais in Thouarce.

A pretty *village fleuri* in the centre of the vineyards, Beaulieu, has a *caveau* which combines wine museum and *hall de dégustation* or tasting room. Beyond the wine villages of St Lambert du Lattay and St Aubin de Luigné, ringed by vine-clad hills, is the agreeable little town of Rochefort sur Loire whose raison d'être is its wine. The acknowledged capital of Coteaux de la Loire wines, it has a safe sandy beach and an orientation table helping you to identify the landmarks in the panoramic views.

One of the most famous parts of the Coteaux are the nearby Quarts de Chaume vineyards, with a perfect exposure to the sun, from which comes a delicious sweet white wine which ages superbly and has a magnificent perfume. The vineyards get their name from the dues that were payable by medieval wine growers to the *seigneur* who owned the land: no less than a quarter of the crop. Chaume wines can be tasted at the Château de Plaisance.

Rochefort is on the Corniche Angevine, a pretty road running midway along the vine-covered slope to Chalonnes, where the Loire divides into three arms to flow between groups of tiny islands linked by bridges. Halfway along the corniche is La Haie Longue, where there are wide views of the valley. From Chalonnes, the most direct way west to Montjean is on the *levée* or dyke road along the left bank of the Loire – though going the long way round through La Pommeraye would give one the opportunity to call at the cellars of a locally appreciated winegrower, M. Boré. West of Montjean, also with a *caveau*, is St-Florent-le-Vieil. It stands on a hill above the left bank of the Loire, and owes its origin to a monastery burned down there in 848 by Charles the Bald – no one knows why. In the parish Church of St Pierre, once part of the abbey, is the splendid tomb carved by the 19th-century sculptor David d'Angers of Charles de Bonchamps. He was the leader of the Royalist uprising against the Revolution who spared the lives of 5,000 Republican prisoners.

An excursion west from St Florent, driving out along the left bank of the Loire and back by the right, takes in a number of interesting villages and towns noted for their wine. It begins by following the Loire downstream on the mainly scenic N751 to Bouzillé, a village in a sylvan setting but with a name always good for a laugh since it means in colloquial French 'shot to pieces'. Near the village is the Chapel of La Bourgonnière, dull and modern outside, magnificently ancient inside, with decorated vaulting, frescoes of the Crucifixion, and ornate statues.

On a hill a few miles west is Liré, *village natal* of Joachim de Bellay, a 16th-century poet who liked 'more than the sea-air, the sweetness of Anjou'. In the village is a museum devoted to the poet and a *caveau de dégustation*. Still on the left bank of the river, the road continues west to Champtoceaux, its main street running along the crest leading to a park with a modern château set among the ruins of a fortified medieval settlement. The promenade of Champalud beside the river is charming.

Across the Loire is Oudun and its massive castle keep, from where the drive back to St Florent passes through vineyards producing the thirst-quenching Muscadet du Coteaux de la Loire and the charming old riverside town of Ancenis before reaching Ingrandes – the eastern gateway to Brittany. After Champtocé, topped by a ruined feudal castle built by Gilles de Laval, companion-in-arms of Joan of Arc, the road leaves the Loire to reach St Georges. Here, in good years, the full and luscious white wines are made from grapes allowed to shrivel on the vine – though the risk is that autumn frosts may ruin them before they are gathered. The well-known Coulée de Serrant *appellation* demands a minimum of 12·5° of alcohol. The great Renaissance mansion known as the Château de Serrant, built by an Irish family with the English-sounding name of Walsh, is flanked by round towers and is well worth visiting if only for a sight of the chapel.

From St Georges, minor roads lead south-east to the straggling village of Savennières beside the wide Loire and to one of the oldest Romanesque churches in Anjou. The wines of Savennières are probably the best of all those produced in the province from the Chenin Blanc grape: fresh and with a distinctive bouquet, they tend to be deliciously dry and strong (12·5°) and take a long time to mature. The three best growths are Roche aux Moines, Château d'Epire, and Coulée de Serrant.

Like the other red wines of Anjou, those from the Roche aux Moines vineyards, centred on a ruined château perched on a spur above the Loire, are virtually unknown outside the region. But the white wines that come from them are famous. That part owned by the sophisticated Madame Joly occupies the site of the battle in 1214, when the army of the Dauphin Louis VIII defeated John Lackland and his men to bring to a close Plantagenet rule in Anjou. Many of the English men-at-arms killed during the battle were buried where they fell. The vineyards of Roche aux Moines have enjoyed their great reputation since 1285, when they were owned by the Abbey of St Nicolas d'Angers. Reached by narrow roads beside the river to the north is Bouchemaine, a port at the junction of the Maine and the Loire, here as broad as a lake.

Astride the Maine, Angers is a well laid-out city of spacious squares and wide boulevards with a relaxed atmosphere unusual for a place of its size. Built of pale-grey stone, it is dominated by the huge castle built by St Louis in the 13th century which incorporates no less than 17 towers (reduced in height when knocked about by Henri III during the religious wars). Their striped appearance comes from being built of alternate layers of stone and slate. Like most of the tiles used for roofing virtually every building in Anjou, the slate was quarried at Trelazé, a suburb on the south-east.

Faded now but still impressive, the Gothic tapestries depicting the Apocalypse which once decorated the interior of the castle are displayed in a specially fitted-out room in the building. Other sights in Angers, where Arthur Wesley, the future Duke of Wellington, was taught to ride a horse, are the many sculptures by David d'Angers in the Logis Barrault and the Ancien Hôpital St Jean, founded by the Plantagenet King Henry II in 1175. Among the exhibits in the wine museum set up in the original cellars of the hospital is a porphyry urn described by its donor, the genial Réné, last Duke of Anjou, as a wine jar used at the marriage feast at Cana in Galilee in biblical times.

Angers and Tours stage their wine fairs simultaneously. Angers is a big, well organised affair and shows all the wines of Anjou. Food is usually confined to a big display of local cheeses. As at most such fairs in France, sampling is free, but Bacchus is usually kept at bay by the business-like atmosphere. The Angers show is the more enjoyable. One reason might be that although they claim to speak the purest French the Tourangeaux are somewhat sparing with words, whereas the Angevins, fond of good living and wine though not the *sac à vins* their neighbours unkindly make them out to be, are more cheerful and open.

# Glossary of wine terms

**Appellation contrôlée**: a guarantee of origin, defining the area where wine is produced and, among other things, the maximum permitted yield and the alcoholic content of the wine.

**Cave, caveau**: cellar, but not necessarily below ground.

**Cépage**: the variety of vine cultivated.

**Chai**: a 'cellar' at ground level, sometimes meaning warehouse.

**Chaptalisation**: adding sugar to the must to increase the alcohol content of the finished wine, forbidden in some wine districts of France.

**Co-operative**: a joint enterprise enabling growers to avoid the often uneconomic expense of making their own wine.

**Coupage**: blending one wine with another to give it more body and flavour.

**Cru**: denotes wine of a specific area and sometimes, as in the Bordelais, an individual growth.

**Cuve close**: secondary fermentation of wine in closed tank.

**Gout de terroir**: having an earthy taste.

**Liquoreux**: describes white wines rich in alcohol and sugar, the one balancing the other.

**Méthode champenoise**: secondary fermentation in bottle.

**Millesimé**: wine of a good year from a specific vineyard or district.

**Négociant**: blender, wholesaler, often wrongly translated as shipper.

**Pourriture noble**: noble rot or botrytis cinerea, a species of yeast which shrivels the skin of the grape and condenses the juice.

**Supérieur**: a term of little value, usually indicating only higher alcohol content.

**Vinage**: adding alcohol to wine, a practice outlawed in France.

**VDQS** (Vin Delimité de Qualité Supérieur): better than average wine from a defined area.

**Vigneron**: vineyard worker, usually meaning working proprietor.

# Where to stay
# Recommended hotels, restaurants, and campsites

Key: (A) luxury (B) medium grade (C) economy

## ALSACE

**Hotels**

Bergheim – à la Vignette: (C), homely *auberge* in heart of vineyards; 12 rooms

Kaysersberg – du Château: (B), friendly welcome; good food; quiet; 12 rooms

Obernai – Diligence: (A), in main square; 30 charming rooms; pleasant restaurant

**Campsites**

Molsheim – Municipal: (15 Mar-Oct), 1 km SE; by river Bruche; shaded; clubroom

Riquewihr – Intercommunal: (May-Sept), 2 km E on D19; level grass; food shop

Selestat – les Cigognes: (Whitsun-Oct), 1 km S off N83; small; central location

## ARMAGNAC

**Hotels**

Auch – France: (A), 40 attractive rooms; one of the best restaurants in the region

Condom – Table des Cordeliers: (A), regional specialities of chef Réné Sandrini

Manciet – Auberge: (C), homely atmosphere; good-value menus; 10 spacious rooms

**Campsites**

Auch – Municipal: (all year), 1 km S on N21; shaded; fishing; bathing; boating

Bretagne d'Armagnac – Lacs Zou-Fou-Dou: (15 June-15 Sept), by lake; restaurant

Lectoure – les 3 Vallées: (Easter-Sept), off N21; by lake; shop; takeaway-meals

## BEAUJOLAIS

**Hotels**

Fleurie – Auberge du Cep: (B), friendly service; booking advisable in evening

Julienas – Chez la Rose: (C), family run; homely atmosphere; good food; 9 rooms

St Lager – Auberge de St Lager: (C), savoury local specialities; 4 simple rooms

**Campsites**
Beaujeu – Municipal: (15 Apr-Sept), central location; small; food shops near by
St Georges de Reneins – Camp de Ludna: (15 Mar-15 Oct), in quiet setting; well run
Villefranche – la Plage: (May-Sept), 3 km E beside Saône; play area; river bathing

## BORDELAIS

**Hotels**
Blaye – Bellevue: (B), quiet situation; 24 modernised rooms; easy parking
Langon – Lion d'Or: (B), 20 rooms (most with shower); noted cuisine
Libourne – Loubat: (B), pleasant atmosphere; good food; 51 rooms, attractive bar
Soulac – Progrès: (C), family run; convenient for Medoc; honest menus; 10 rooms
**Campsites**
Creon – Bel Air: (all year), 2 km NW on N671; quiet; shaded; food shop in season
Fronsac – Le Fronsadais: (6 Jun-Oct), in village beside Dordogne; bathing; boating
Langon – Allées Marines: (Jun-15 Sept), pretty setting near Garonne; boating
Soulac – Palace: (Easter-Sept), on northern tip of Medoc; spacious; near beach

## BURGUNDY

**Hotels**
Beaune – Poste: (A), ancient hotel now modernised; notable restaurant; 25 rooms
Dijon – Terminus: (B), agreeable atmosphere; good food at sensible prices; 30 pleasant rooms
Fixin – Chez Jeannette: (C), family-run *auberge*; copious honest menus; 11 rooms
**Campsites**
Beaune – les Cent Vignes: (Apr-Oct), quiet situation; food shop; clubhouse; shaded
Meursault – Grappe d'Or: (Apr-15 Oct), N on D111E; pleasant setting; part terraced
Premeaux-Prissey – Moulin de Prissey: (Easter-Oct), E on D115E; small and quiet

## CHAMPAGNE

**Hotels**
Champillon – Royal Champagne: (A), converted coaching inn; superb food; 14 rooms

Epernay – Berceaux: (B), central situation; specialities of region; 33 rooms
Vinay – Briquetterie: (B), newly built; comfortable; notable restaurant;
42 rooms
**Campsites**
Dormans – Essi Plage: (Easter-Sept), Route de Vincelles; peaceful; beside
Marne
Epernay – Municipal: (Mar-Oct), 1 km NW on Cumières road; shaded;
boating; fishing
Reims – Camp du Champagne: (Easter-Sept), 3 km SE on N44; food shop
in season

## COGNAC
**Hotels**
Barbezieux – Boule d'Or: (A), central; renowned for regional dishes; 28
rooms
Jarnac – Terminus: (B), family-run; restaurant popular with locals; 15
rooms
Pons – Auberge Pontoise: (B), central; friendly welcome; garden; 26 small
rooms
**Campsites**
Cognac – Municipal: (Jun-Sept), 2 km N on D24, beside Charente; bathing;
fishing
Saintes – Municipal: (15 May-15 Oct), 1 km N on D128; swimming pool;
clubhouse

## JURA
**Hotels**
Arbois – Paris: (A), central; friendly atmosphere; imaginative menus; 21
rooms
Lons le Saunier – Cheval Rouge: (B), coaching inn updated; 16 modernised
rooms
Poligny – Paris: (C), welcoming; tasty regional dishes in restaurant; 27
rooms
**Campsites**
Arbois – Municipal: (May-Sept), E off D107; level grass; quiet; shop in
season
Baume les Messieurs – la Toupe: (Apr-Sept), shaded; beside river Seille;
boating
Lons le Saunier – la Marjorie: (15 Jun-Sept), spacious; play area; food shop

## LOIRE
**Hotels**
Chenehutte les Tuffeaux – Hostellerie du Prieuré: (A), in park by Loire;
28 rooms
Ingrandes – Lion d'Or: (B), noted restaurant; 21 rooms; garden; easy
parking

Rosiers, les – Auberge Jeanne de Laval: (A), best restaurant in region; 10 rooms

Tours – Bordeaux: (B), modernised in good taste; central situation; 54 rooms

**Campsites**

Azay le Rideau – Parc du Sabot: (23 Mar-Sept), pleasant setting beside Indre

Ingrandes – le Port: (Easter-Sept), small; beside Loire; shaded; boating; fishing

Saumur – Municipal: (all year), on island in river; food shop; clubhouse; quiet

## PROVENCE

**Hotels**

Croix Valmer – de la Mer: (A), in garden setting with swimming pool; 32 rooms

Draguinan – Col de l'Ange: (B), new hotel on outskirts; 29 rooms all with bath

Vidauban – Le Logis du Guetteur: (B), panoramic dining room; 11 modern rooms

**Campsites**

Cavalaire – de la Baie: (Mar-Sept), quiet wooded setting; central; takeaway-meals

Draguinan – la Foux: (all year), children's swimming pool; food shop; TV room

Grimaud – de la Plage: (May-Sept), on sandy beach facing St Tropez; spacious

Pierrefeu – les Défends de Bécasson: (all year), quiet; food shop; play area

## RHONE

**Hotels**

Châteauneuf du Pape – Mule du Pape: (A), panoramic restaurant; best in the area

Condrieu – Beau Rivage: (A), nicely sited above Rhône; excellent food; 28 rooms

St Peray – des Bains: (B), in pleasant location; attractive garden; 35 rooms

**Campsites**

Albon – Senaud: (Mar-Nov), 1 km S off D122; in grounds of château; shop; bar

Condrieu – Bel 'Epoque: (May-Oct), beside Rhône; takeaway-meals; clubhouse; shop

Orange – Colline St Eutrope: (Apr-Oct), on hill above Roman theatre; small

Tournon – Municipal: (Feb-Nov), beside river Doux; shaded; play area; river bathing